TaylorED Time Workbook

How to Be the Captain of Your Character's Creation

ANDREW S. TAYLOR

With Professional Photography
by CAROLE A. FLETCHER

PEAK PRESS

An Imprint for GracePoint Publishing (www.GracePointPublishing.com)

GracePoint Matrix, LLC

624 S. Cascade Ave, Suite 201, Colorado Springs, CO 80903

www.GracePointMatrix.com

Email: Admin@GracePointMatrix.com

SAN # 991-6032

A Library of Congress Control Number has been requested and is pending.

ISBN: (Paperback) 978-1-955272-41-4

eISBN: 978-1-955272-44-5

Books may be purchased for educational, business, or sales promotional use.
For bulk order requests and price schedule contact:
Orders@GracePointPublishing.com

DEDICATION

Love & Gratitude!!

Love-A-Lot, Lifetime, Family & Friends

It is with my fully felt, whole heart, I say to all who love and support me,

THANK YOU!!

A+

"We do not believe in ourselves until someone reveals that deep inside us something is valuable, worth listening to, worthy of our trust, sacred to our touch. Once we believe in ourselves, we can risk curiosity, wonder, spontaneous delight or any experience that reveals the human spirit."

E. E. Cummings

TABLE OF CONTENTS

THOUGHTS FOR TODAY—REPRINTED

Self-Help Books: Any one (book) will do and anyone (you) can do. My questions are "Will you impose your will?" and "Will you do your life's work?" I hope this one (book) and someone (you) will work for you. My unique approach with this book is how it parallels the same concepts and techniques used to build fictional characters in theater, TV, and movies with the building of non-fictional, real-life, everyday characters and people, a.k.a. *YOU!*

Question: If theater, TV, and movie artists, actors, and actresses can *magically* create whole new *fictional* characters and worlds, then why can't you also apply a little bit of your own MAGIC (Make A Good Intelligent Choice), and create a whole new, *non-fictional YOU?*

Answer: I believe you can. And I believe you will... *only if....* You will achieve this result *only if* you totally commit to a practical process of personal growth, just like the one presented in this book. If you complete this journey successfully, then you will have positively produced your greatest masterpiece. You will have consciously created your *new and improved, real-life character.* And you will have MAGIC-ally manifested, your fully FANTASTIC (Full And Novel, Thriving And Successful, Totally In Control), self-helped self.

One Word's Definition: *holistic* [adj.] involving all of something; someone's all-encompassing everything. This includes all of someone's physical, intellectual, emotional, spiritual, solo, and social situations. This word commonly refers to using unusual, healthy, healing methodologies, i.e. practicing *holistic* medicine. But in this book, I abundantly apply this word to alternative applications and unconventional contexts.

This is an additional Thought For Today. With its inclusion, it is my intention, to begin the workbook with a life affirming energy of intrinsic inspiration.

"Your work is to discover your work, and with all your heart dedicate your life to it completely." ~ Buddha

So as you use this workbook, make yourself a 100% guaranteed, promissory commitment of a lifetime. "I do hereby solemnly swear and positively promise: I will do my life's work."

THOUGHTS FOR TODAY—TAKE TWO

"A journey of a thousand miles begins and ends with just one step." ~ Lao Tzu

Think your morning JUICE (Journaling Ultimately Inspirational Character Evolution). Take your first steps. Answer the following questions: "What are your first impressions of the Thoughts for Today in the book and the workbook?" "Why are you reading this book and workbook?" "What do you hope to find as you travel on your New Life Adventure: A Journey of Self-Discovery?" For today's journal entry, think about these questions for a few minutes and write your answers.

Date: _____/_____/_____

What are your first impressions of the Thoughts for Today?

Book's Thoughts?

_____

_____

_____

_____

_____

Workbook's Thoughts?

_____

_____

_____

_____

_____

_____

Why are you reading this book and workbook?

_____

_____

_____

_____

_____

_____

What do you hope to find, as you travel on your New Life Adventure: A Journey of Self-Discovery?

_____

_____

_____

_____

_____

_____

TAYLORED TIME ACRONYMS

In this book you will find an abundance of acronyms. Use this list any time you need to know what one means.

BEAUTIFUL: Be yourself, Enlightened, Alive, Unique, Trustworthy, Intelligent, Faithful, and Unconditionally Loving!

EAT: Eat A Treat!

FANTASTIC: Full And Novel, Thriving And Successful, Totally In Control!

FEAR: False Expectations Apparent Realities

FUEL: Full-filling and Unconditionally and Enthusiastically Love

GIGSS: Gather In Group Support Systems

JUICE: Journaling Ultimately Inspirational Character Evolution

LAB: Life Appreciation Break

LRM: Lifetime Role Models

LOVE: Lots of Vulnerable Emotions! Lots of Vibrant Energies!

MAGIC: Make A Good Intelligent Choice

MINE: Moment Immortal Never Ending!

PIES: Physical Intellectual Emotional Spiritual

SOUL: Spirit Of Ultimate LOVE!

SORT: Self Occupations Relationships Time-Transitions

INTRODUCTION

All right, "Action!" This is the *TaylorED Time Workbook: How to Be the Captain of Your Character's Creation*. Think of this as your ship's log as you navigate the *TaylorED Time: How to Dramatically Build Your Character & Live the Life FANTASTIC!* book. I also wanted to title it I Captain, My Captain: The, "I Am the Captain of my Character's Creation" and the "I am Doing the Work" Workbook. Make these two titles your daily determinations and life affirmations.

This workbook is designed for two purposes. The first is to give you the extra space you need to complete and/or redo all the book's exercises. The second is to show you how to begin, and keep, a character creation, lifetime journal. This is an invaluable tool for personal growth and real self-improvement.

To help accomplish this second purpose, you will draw inspiration from special, section-specific quotes, original poetry, and positively picturesque, professional photography. Then you will describe your inspired thoughts and feelings. This way you will proficiently record your progress, as you tenaciously travel through the process presented in the book. This is truly and tangibly living the life FANTASTIC!

To begin a character creation lifetime journal, you simply have to think things up and write them down. When you are routinely able to perform this productive practice every time inspiration evokes contemplation, then you will effectively be able to efficiently keep a character creation lifetime journal.

After you read each special, section specific quote, or original poetry, or you view one of the positively picturesque, professional photographs, take a small dramatic pause, or beat. Then, "Think your morning JUICE. (Journaling Ultimately Inspirational Character Evolution). Do what others do when they keep a daily diary. Record all the noteworthy, inspired thoughts and feelings of your life. This way you will be Journaling Ultimately Inspirational Character Evolution.

THE 16 SECRETS OF SUCCESS —REPRINTED

1. Holistically know yourself.

2. Find true (for you) north. Define your dreams and goals.

3. Use creative visualization. Make conscious choices. Map your projected life plan. Write everything down.

4. Take action immediately. Remember the NIKE slogan and Just Do It™.

5. Focus and pay attention.

6. Ask for help. Gratefully accept help. And earn all the help you are given.

7. How you think is everything. Eliminate negatives. Think only positives.

8. Be a lifelong learner.

9. Learn to see and analyze all life's little details. Learn from your mistakes. Follow the flow until all life lessons are learned.

10. Organize your life. Find a system that works for you.

11. Create a clear picture of the world. See how it is all connected.

12. Adjust your attitude. Empower your passion. Eliminate forecasting FEARs (False Expectations Apparent Realities)! Do what FUELs (Full-filling Unconditionally Enthusiastically Love) you!

13. Be perceptive from your perspective! Be persistent to your purpose! Never settle for *only* content and comfortable. *Also,* always strive for holistically happy and hungry! *Never give up! … Don't quit! … EVER!*

14. Get GIGSS (Gather In Group Support Systems). Take total responsibility for your life. Make a commitment to playing the lead-er part of *Your Life!* Live your life so self-improvement and acts of altruism are synonymous!

15. Celebrate family and friends! Create unity and community! Tap into your SOUL (Spirit Of Ultimate LOVE (Living Only Vibrant Energies))! Live the Life FANTASTIC (Full And Novel, Thriving And Successful, Totally In Control)!

16. Presentize yourself! Go back to number one. Start over!

THE 16 SECRETS OF SUCCESS —TAKE TWO

"You don't need to see the whole staircase. Take the first step on faith."
~ Martin Luther King Jr.

Think your morning JUICE. Putting your thoughts and feelings in writing are your first steps, and you need to know it's usually the most difficult step to take. It's easy to only think about it, but actually doing it can be the hardest part of the whole journey. For today's workbook activity, read each of The 16 Secrets of Success and write your first impressions.

Date: _____/_____/_____

1) Holistically know yourself.

_____

_____

_____

_____

2) Determine your true north dreams and goals.

_____

_____

_____

_____

3) Use creative visualization. Make conscious choices. Map your projected life plan. Write everything down.

_____

_____

_____

_____

4) Take action immediately. Remember the NIKE slogan and Just Do It™.

_____

_____

_____

_____

5) Focus and pay attention.

_____

_____

_____

_____

6) Ask for help. Gratefully accept help. And earn all the help you are given.

_____

_____

_____

_____

7) How you think is everything. Eliminate negatives. Think only positives.

_____

_____

_____

_____

8) Be a lifelong learner.

_____

_____

_____

_____

9) Learn to see and analyze all life's little details. Learn from your mistakes. Follow the flow until all life lessons are learned.

_____

_____

_____

_____

10) Organize your life. Find a system which works for you.

_____

_____

_____

_____

11) Create a clear picture of the world. See how it is all connected.

_____

_____

_____

_____

12) Adjust your attitude. Empower your passion. Eliminate forecasting FEARs (False Expectations Apparent Realities)! Do what FUELs (Full-filling Unconditionally Enthusiastically Love) you!

_____

_____

_____

_____

13) Be perceptive from your perspective! Be persistent to your purpose! Never settle for *only* content and comfortable. *Also,* always strive for holistically happy and hungry! *Never give up! … Don't quit! … EVER!*

_____

_____

_____

_____

14) Get GIGSS (Gather In Group Support Systems). Take total responsibility for your life. Make a commitment to playing the lead-er part of *Your Life!* Live your life so self-improvement and acts of altruism are synonymous!

_____

_____

_____

_____

15) Celebrate family and friends! Create unity and community! Tap into your SOUL (Spirit Of Ultimate LOVE (Living Only Vibrant Energies))! Live the Life FANTASTIC (Full And Novel, Thriving And Successful, Totally In Control)!

_____

_____

_____

_____

16) Presentize yourself! Go back to number one. Start over!

_____

_____

_____

_____

A GUIDE FOR
HOW TO USE THIS WORKBOOK

Step 1: Read the special, section-specific quote, the original poetry piece, the additional thought-provoking text, and/or view the positively picturesque, professional photography.

Step 2: Think your morning JUICE. Describe your inspired thoughts and feelings and write whatever the writing prompts encourage you to write. If you want, do free association writing; after all it's free.

Step 3: When you arrive at an exercise page, once again write what the writing prompts encourage you to write or write whatever you want to write in the extra blank space.

Note: The workbook is organized with the same section headings as the book. This way both Table of Contents match, and you can easily find whichever section you need. Also, don't forget whenever you need extra space, copy A Blank Page from the back of this workbook and insert it wherever you need it.

Okay. Now turn the page. Our journey is about to begin.

CHAPTER 1:
CHARACTER CRYSTALLIZATION!

Preview

"If you want to change the world, *you* are the easiest place to start." ~ Andrew S. Taylor

Think your morning JUICE. With this quote, we will start Chapter 1: Character Crystallization! For today's journal entry, list up to twelve self-character traits you'd like to change. Then answer the following questions: "Why did you choose these specific self-character traits?" and "When you make these changes, how will your life, and your world, change?"

Date: _____/_____/_____

List up to twelve self-character traits you'd like to change.

1) _____

_____

2) _____

_____

3) _____

_____

4) _____

_____

5) _____

_____

6) _____

_____

7) _____

_____

8) _____

_____

9) _____

_____

10) _____

_____

11) _____

_____

12) _____

_____

Why did you choose these specific self-character traits?

1) _____

_____

2) _____

_____

3) _____

_____

4) _____

_____

5) _____

_____

6) _____

_____

7) _____

_____

8) _____

_____

9) _____

_____

10) _____

_____

11) _____

_____

12) _____

_____

When you make these changes, how will your life, and your world, change?

_____

_____

_____

_____

_____

_____

_____

_____

_____

_____

_____

"When I change myself, I change the whole world." ~ Gloria Anzaldua

Think your morning JUICE. Continue writing on this idea. For today's journal entry, answer the question below.

Date: ____/____/____

When I change myself, how does the whole world change? Be specific.

_____

_____

_____

_____

_____

_____

_____

_____

_____

_____

_____

_____

_____

"Change and growth will only take place when a person takes a risk and dares to experiment with their own life." ~ Herbert Otto

Think your morning JUICE. I'm including this quote because it's a subtle promise. By choosing to read this book, do all the exercises, and conscientiously and consistently keep the workbook journal, you choose to be "a person (who) takes a risk and dares to experiment with (your) own life." I say congratulations and good choice! I hope the resulting change and growth in your life will be everything you dream it to be, and a whole lot more! For today's journal entry, describe a couple of your future dreams and ambitions.

Date: _____/_____/_____

Describe a couple of your future dreams and ambitions.

1) _____

_____

_____

_____

_____

_____

2) _____

_____

_____

_____

_____

_____

Character and Self-Inventory

"Open your mind, heart, and arms, and take it all in." ~ Kobi Yamada

Think your morning JUICE. Great! You've started writing, and you have a little mental momentum. For today's journal entry, keep writing and answer the questions, "Are you open-minded?" and "How?" Apply your answers to The Small Picture of specifically reading, learning, and potentially benefiting from this particular self-help book and also to The Big Picture of being open minded about life in general.

Date: ____/____/____

Are you open-minded? How?

The Small Picture?

_____

_____

_____

_____

The Big Picture?

_____

_____

_____

_____

"You must be the change you wish to see in the world." ~ Mahatma Gandhi

Think your morning JUICE. There is an anecdote, which goes with Gandhi's quote. One day a very concerned mother asked Gandhi if he would intervene on her behalf and counsel her son to please stop eating so much processed sugar and unhealthy junk food. Gandhi said, "Come back to me in two weeks and I will tell you if I can help." When the two weeks were over the perplexed parent returned to hear Gandhi's answer. He said, "Yes. Now I can tell him to stop eating processed sugar."

The mother asked, "Why did you have to wait two weeks?"

Gandhi said, "Two weeks ago I was eating processed sugar. Now I am not." I highly recommend the movie *Gandhi* to learn more about his life and his teachings.

For today's journal entry, keep this anecdote in mind and answer the questions, "Do you practice what you preach?" and "Do you possess all the character traits you want others to associate with you?" If not, what are your top two areas which need improving? If yes, what are your top two areas of character consistency and strength?

Date: ____/____/____

Do you practice what you preach? Do you possess all the character traits you want others to associate with you? If not, what are your top two areas, which need improving? If yes, what are your top two areas of character consistency and strength?

1) _____

_____

_____

_____

_____

_____

2) _____

_____

_____

_____

_____

_____

Andrewism: Ladies and Gentlemen, That's The News!

Ladies and Gentlemen,
This Just In: A Tidal Wave, Flash Flood, Hit A Coastal-Residential Area Today.
The Total Extent Of Damage And Devastation: One Home And One Family, Destroyed.
Two Children Were Killed When Waves Of Water Crushed And Drowned Them As They Slept.
Two Parents Were Devastated When They Discovered The Mid-Day, Nightmareic Scene.
They Had Just Returned Home From A Successful Food-Gathering Flight.
For The Rest Of Their Days, The Only Song They Will Sing,
Will Be The Song Of The Dead And The Gone.

Ladies & Gentleman,
The Costal Area Was A Roof's Rain Gutter.
The Residents Who Lived There Were Birds.
The Water Came From A Misguided Child.
The All-Too-Soon-To-Be-Adult Was Armed
With A Fully Loaded Garden Hose And A Nozzle Gun!

Ladies & Gentleman,
For Me, It Is More Disturbing
If These Last Bits Of Information,
Make This Story Less Disturbing For You.

Ladies & Gentleman,
That's The Way It Is.
That's The News As It Was Today.
Hopefully Someday, We'll Realize, It Doesn't Have to Be This Way.
Hopefully It's Simply A Matter Of Believing It Will.
Hopefully It's Simply A Matter Of, … "It Will" Power!

Ladies & Gentleman,
This Journey Towards This Place In Our Hopefully Near Future
Starts With One Person Taking An Action Step.

That Person Could Be You.   That Person Should Be You.
Do Not Leave It Up To Chance.   Make A Choice.
Be That Person   Now!

Ladies & Gentleman,   Thank You For Tuning In.
Good Night, That's The News,   As It Will Be Tomorrow.

Think your morning JUICE. The amazing anecdote associated with this *Andrewism* poetry piece describes how I actually saw this terribly tragic event take place. I was working as a golf caddy and we were all sitting around waiting for our turn to be matched with a group. Six kids were playing basketball and four were playing cards. Suddenly, I saw past them all, and I unwontedly witnessed the "Misguided Child" shoot the spray of water at the bird's nest. I quickly confronted him and alarmingly asked, "Why did you do it?" His incredibly ignorant, cold-hearted response was, "I was just cleaning the gutters?" I tried to tell him how the gutters were in fact the bird's home but this point of view didn't seem to faze the "All-To-Soon-To-Be-Adult."

I was then matched with a foursome, and I spent the next four hours externally being a caddy and internally processing what I'd just distressingly experienced. When I returned to the clubhouse, I grabbed my pen and notepad, and I wrote this poetry piece. I knew it was the only way my mind would ever be at peace.

What do you think? What are your initial thoughts and feelings? What would you have done if you were the child? How would you have responded if you were the witness? What are your thoughts and feelings on the rest of the poetry piece? If you had to write a poetry piece, or a "tell it like it is" candid commentary, news article, about the event, what would you write? For today's journal entry, answer these questions.

Date: _____/_____/_____

What do you think? What are your initial thoughts and feelings?

_____

_____

_____

_____

What would you have done if you were the child?

_____

_____

_____

_____

How would you have responded if you were the witness?

_____

_____

_____

_____

What are your thoughts and feelings on the rest of the poetry piece?

_____

_____

_____

_____

If you had to write a poetry piece, or a tell-it-like-it-is candid commentary, news article about the event, what would you write?

Title: _____

_____

_____

_____

_____

_____

_____

_____

_____

_____

_____

_____

_____

_____

_____

_____

"The one who knows others is wise. The one who knows the self is enlightened." ~ Lao Tzu

Think your morning JUICE. This quote raises an important question, "What does it mean to know yourself?" For today's journal entry, write your answer.

Date: ____/____/____

What does it mean to know yourself?

_____

_____

_____

_____

"I always wanted to be somebody. I should have been more specific." ~ Lily Tomlin

Think your morning JUICE. Whenever I hear "Who do you think you are?" whether it's directed at me or not, internally, I always answer the question. I look with my mind's eye, and I see the big picture of who I am today. This image leads me to imagine who I want to be tomorrow, and every time I engage in this delicious daydream, my ambitions get bigger, and the delightful depictions of my foreseeable future get more specific. So I ask you, "Who do you think you are today?" and "Who do you imagine you will be tomorrow?" Be specific.

Date: ____/____/____

Who do you think you are today?

_____

_____

_____

_____

Who do you imagine you will be tomorrow? Be specific.

_____

_____

_____

_____

"Thoroughly to know oneself, is above all art. In fact, it is the highest art." ~ Author Unknown

Think your morning JUICE. On a scale of one to ten how well do you know yourself? One is an amnesia victim, who keeps asking, "Who am I?" Ten is the same as if you were an all knowing, all seeing, super being. For today's journal entry, answer the question and explain your answer. Then list a few ideas how to improve your present day, self-knowledge score.

Date: ____/____/____

On a scale of one to ten how well do you know yourself? _____

Why do you score yourself with this number?

_____

_____

_____

_____

List a few ideas how to improve your present day, self-knowledge score.

1) _____

_____

2) _____

_____

3) _____

_____

4) _____

_____

"Acting is filling in all the white space on the page." ~ Konstantin Stanislavski

Think your morning JUICE. This quote is taken directly from the book section, and it is still the best explanation of acting I've heard. For today's journal entry, write your definition and explanation of acting and write about any parallels you see between acting and real life.

Date: ____/____/____

Write your definition and explanation of acting. Describe any parallels you see between acting and real life.

_____

_____

_____

_____

Part One: Nature vs. Nurture

Andrewism: Life: A Convergence Of Conversations

How Did I Get Here? Why Am I Here?
    (Physical)   Preview The Path And Look Back In Love.
    (Intellectual)   Check Out The Education Records And Read Between The Lines.
        There Is Where You'll Find The Real Tell Tale Truth.
        After All, We Know There's A Grand Canyon Gap Between Book Smart And Street Smart.
        And We All Know, "Common Sense Is Not So Common."
    (Emotional)   For Sure, Thanks Be To Mom And Dad!
        Because of You, My Heart Is Glad!
        Deep Down, All The Way To The Core!
        Because Of You, I Know What My Heart Is For!
    (Spiritual)   Now There Is Where The Bonus Round Is Sure To Be Found!
DAD - My, "Founding Father," Says In Conversation, "We Are Only Containers For DNA."
        Okay Granted, This Is A Very Basic "Natural Nature," "Boat-In-A-Bottle," Belief System.
        It's One Man's Semantic Description Of Our Human Conditional Situation.
Let's See, As I Understand It,
        We're A, "Boat-At-Sea," And, "Sea-Men," "Board," A, "She-Ship,"
        And Thus Our Journey Boldly Begins.
Two Types Of Trips Are Possible:
1) Those Who Travel Under A, "Starless Sky," And Sail With An, "Unconscious Compass."
These Soul-Less Wanderers Find They've Become An, "Isolated Island."
They Are A Solo Cast Away, Lost At Sea.
2) Those Who Travel On, "Common Course Currents," And With An Accurately Made Map,
They Set Sail With Determination, In Search Of Their, "Destiny's Destination."
These Soul-Full Wonderers Find They Have Begetted A "Collective Community."
This, "Holistic Home," Is The Best Of All Possible Containers.

12

MOM - My, "Mother Nature," Says In Conversation,
"More Often Than Not, Your Attitude, Not Your Aptitude, Will Determine Your Altitude."
~ Zig Zigler
 Okay Granted, This Is A Very Basic "Natural Nurturer," "Positive-Perspective," Belief System.
 It's One Woman's Semantic Description Of Our Human Conditional Situation.
Let's See, As I Understand It,
 In Order To Reach Your, "Self's Summit," You Must Empower Yourself!
 Your Aptitude, AKA Your Talents, Needs The Fuel Of Passionate, Enthusiastic Energy,
 To Achieve Your Ultimate Altitude.
 This Is The Life Blood Of Being Absolutely Alive!
Two Types Of Trips Are Possible:
1) The Negative, Reactionist, Is Destined To Descend And Spiral Down The Path,
Until They Quietly Quit, Literally!
2) The Positive, Pro-Activist, Is Destined To Ascend And Spiral Up The Path,
Until They Wonderfully Win, "A Lived Life," AKA, "The Prize Of Peace!"
 Okay, Now I Can Answer My Questions!
 You See, I Have Talked With These Two Teachers At Great Length!
 They Are My Answers!
 They Are My How And Why I Am Here!
 I Am Their Collective Creation!
 I Am Their Positive Production!
 They Are My Soul's Foundation!
 I Am A Convergence Of Conversations!

Think your morning JUICE. I wrote this *Andrewism* poetry piece, to show my appreciation for the incalculable contribution my parents have made in my life. For today's journal entry, think about your parents or guardians, and write your own piece. Use a favorite format. I use poetry. Write your piece either, "FOR MY EYES ONLY!", or choose to share it with your parents or guardians on some special, sentimental occasion.

Date: ____/____/____

Write your own piece, which is inspired by your parents or guardians.

  Title:_____

_____

_____

_____

_____

_____

_____

_____

_____

_____

_____

_____

_____

"Nature makes artists, it teaches them their right mode of expression." ~ Oscar Wilde

Think your morning JUICE. Consider this quote. How does it apply to you? For today's journal entry, list a few of your own genetically inherited talents. Then describe how you manifest and express these talents?

Date: ____ / ____ / ____

List some of your genetically inherited talents.

1) _____

2) _____

3) _____

4) _____

How do you manifest and express these talents?

1) _____

_____

2) _____

_____

3) _____

_____

4) _____

_____

Think your morning JUICE. Here's a creative quickie. If you had to pick a title for this picture, what would it be? For example, my idea is Fun Family Tree! If there's a short story, which explains why you choose your title, please write it.

Title:_____

Date: ____/____/____

Please write your title tale, short story.

_____

_____

_____

_____

_____

_____

"Analyze your life in terms of its environment. Ask if the things around you are helping you toward success, or are they holding you back?" ~ W. Clement Stone

Think your morning JUICE. This quote is perfect for this section. It tells you what to do and it gives you a perfect prompting question. For today's journal entry, do the task and answer the question. Explain the how and why of your answer.

Date: ____/____/____:

Are the things around you helping you toward success, or are they holding you back?

Helping _____ Holding Back _____

How? Why?

_____

_____

_____

_____

_____

_____

"Any technique which increases self-knowledge, should in principle, increase one's creativity." ~ Abraham Maslow

Think your morning JUICE. This quote preempts Exercise 1 in the book. For today's journal entry, write if you think the quote is true or not. Explain why. Then look at the photograph and describe your inspired thoughts and feelings.

Date: _____ / _____ / _____

Write if you think the quote is true or not. Explain why.

_____

_____

_____

_____

_____

_____

Look at the photograph and describe your inspired thoughts and feelings.

_____

_____

_____

_____

_____

_____

Exercise 1 - Nature vs. Nurture: Pre-Script and Life History

Think your morning JUICE. Use this page to continue or redo Exercise 1. Then, when you have completed the exercise, describe your inspired thoughts and feelings.

Date: _____ / _____ / _____

_____

_____

_____

_____

_____

_____

Andrewism: I Want My Life MINEs (Moment Immortal Never Ending!)

Human History Is Full Of MINEs.

There Are Two Kinds.
Both Are Remembered Forever, In The Mind's Eye Of Their Beholder And Their Beheld.

The First Kind Of MINE. Is The Visible Kind.
(Sports & Games - Arts & Entertainment - Politics & Press) The Examples Are Endless.

Through Multi-Media's, Multi-Faceted Lenses The Public Eyes Watch,
Everything That Happens In Our Three-Ring Circus World.
After All, It Is US, And We Love To Watch Ourselves In Our Own Magical, Human-Made Mirrors.
The Result Of Our Society Self Scrutinizing Its' Public People's Many MINEs, Has A Name.
It Is Fame.
It Develops And Then Envelopes Every Soul Which Swallows It Whole.
Everyone Of These Individuals Is Impaled On, Or, Nobly Knighted By,
Its' Double Edged, And Double-Sided Sword.

Okay. Now This Is The Nature Of The Larger-Than-Life, World Wide, Mass Publicized, MINEs.
But What About The Other Kind Of MINEs?
The Second Kind Of MINE Is The Invisible Kind.
For Every Visible MINE There Are An Infinite Number Of Invisible MINEs.
The Masses Never See These And They're Only Remembered By The Mind's Eye Of,
The Select Few, Who Happen To, Experience Them Firsthand.
They're Only Shared By, You And I, Alone.
The Human Doing's, Private Eyes, Who Do This Specialized Seeing,
Become For Each Invisible MINE.,
A Customized Beholder, And A Personalized Beheld.

Okay. So Now You Know The Two Kinds Of MINEs.
I'm Sure Your Question For Our Together Time Is,
"What Should I Do With This New Knowledge?"

I Say Today, Lay Down A Course For An Invisible MINE. Share One With Someone Special.
Do This Day Out And Day In, Everyday. Then With Time, You Can Win, The Prize.
Which In Its Very Name, Says It Is Something Worthy Of Possession.
You Will Find Fame, Within Your Own, Visa-In-Visible, MINE.

Think your morning JUICE. For today's journal entry, read the *Andrewism* poetry piece, and describe your inspired thoughts and feelings. Then list a few MINEs, which were heroically done for you and, (A) List a few MINEs, which you altruistically performed for someone else and (B) Describe how these events changed your life.

Date: _____/_____/_____

Read this *Andrewism* poetry piece, and describe your inspired thoughts and feelings.

_____

_____

_____

_____

List a few MINEs, which were done for you.

1A) _____

2A) _____

3A) _____

4A) _____

List a few MINEs, which you performed for someone else.

1B) _____

2B) _____

3B) _____

4B) _____

Describe how these events changed your life.

1A)_____

_____

2A)_____

_____

3A)_____

_____

4A)_____

_____

1B)_____

_____

2B)_____

_____

3B)_____

_____

4B)_____

_____

Part Two: Fact Foundation PIES Chart

"You'd be surprised how much it cost, to look this cheap." ~ Dolly Parton

Think your morning JUICE. Dolly Parton: This blond-wigged, mega-made-up, surgery-enhanced, country-western, super-star singer is a prime example of, "Don't judge a book by its cover." For today's journal entry, list a few favorite famous and public people who are equal examples of the quote's concept. Explain how these celebrities qualify (A), compare and contrast their external image versus what you know about their internal character traits (B), and explain why these people are on your list of favorites (C).

Date: ____/____/____

List a few favorite famous and public people who are equal examples of the quote's concept.

1)_____   3)_____

2)_____   4)_____

Do the writing prompts for A, B, and C.

1A)_____

_____

1B)_____

_____

1C)_____

_____

2A)_____

_____

2B)_____

_____

2C)_____

_____

3A)_____

_____

3B)_____

_____

3C)_____

_____

4A)_____

_____

4B)_____

_____

4C)_____

_____

Extra Expressings and Thoughtful Thinkings: On the line below, write about how this concept would apply to your character if you were the celebrity of your day dreams.

_____

_____

_____

_____

_____

_____

_____

_____

_____

_____

_____

_____

"Many individuals have, like uncut diamonds, shining qualities beneath a rough exterior."
~ Author Unknown

Think your morning JUICE. The subject of this quote is diamonds-in-the-rough. For today's journal entry, list a few favorite un-famous and private people who are equal examples of the quote's concept. Explain how these people qualify and explain why they are on your list of favorites. Include yourself on the list if the shoe fits.

List a few favorite un-famous and private people who are examples of the quote's concept.

1) _____

2) _____

3) _____

4) _____

Explain how these people qualify and explain why they are on your list of favorites.

1) _____

_____

_____

_____

2) _____

_____

_____

_____

3) _____

_____

_____

_____

4) _____

_____

_____

_____

"Conformity is the jailer of freedom and the enemy of growth." ~ John F. Kennedy

Think your morning JUICE. For today's journal entry, take a good, long look at yourself. The question of the day is, "Are you a conformist?" Answer this question both in regards to specific items such as how you look and dress and also in general with your life philosophy?

Date: ____/____/____

Are you a conformist in regard to specific items? No. _____Yes. _____ How?

_____

_____

_____

_____

Are you a conformist in general with your life philosophy? No. _____Yes. _____ How?

_____

_____

_____

_____

Andrewism: Why Must It Rhyme All The Time?

If I Might,	For A Moment,	Step Into The Light.
If I May,	For Today,	I Have Something To Say.
I Am A Poet.	I Know It.	I Do Not Need To Show It Off, With Rhyme.

My Message Is Clear And Kind.   So Open Up Your Ears And Mind,   Me.
Humanity Needs Tranquility   And Gentility.
The Dove And The Leaf:

These Are Symbols For Love And Peace.   These Need To Increase.
To Us,   This Is Obvious.
That's It In A Nut Shell.   But,   Oh Well,

I Digress From What I Wish To Address.
I Am Speaking Of The Message Container.
I Am Keeping It On Retainer.

My Question In My Poem Mine,   "Why Must It Rhyme All The Time?"
Do You;   Listen Better,   With Appetite Wetter?
Do You,   The Audience,   Go And Show, More Compliance?

Whatever The Case   There Is No Need To Erase.
My Message   Has Been Given.
It's Now Up to You.   Do Your Own Liven.

Note   And I Quote.   Make Yourself Aware And Take Care.
You   And Your World   Will   Thank You, In The End.

Think your morning JUICE. This *Andrewism* poetry piece, is my slightly confrontational and certainly controversial response to the question, "Is it poetry if it unconventionally rhymes or if it does not rhyme at all?"

For today's journal entry, write your thoughts and feelings in response to this question? If you are so inclined, write your own poetry piece, which expresses your position on the matter (A). Or make a copy of your favorite poetry piece (B), and explain why you like it (C). Specifically refer to the poem's degree of conformity or non-conformity, in regard to the standard rules of poetry writing (D).

Date: ____/____/____

Do you think it's poetry if it unconventionally rhymes or if it does not rhyme at all? No. _____Yes. ____ Why?

_____

_____

(A) ___ or (B) ___   Title: _____

_____

_____

_____

_____

_____

_____

_____

_____

_____

_____

_____

_____

(C)_____

_____

(D)_____

_____

"Curiosity is one of the permanent and certain characteristics of a vigorous intellect."
~ Samuel Johnson

Think your morning JUICE. I believe curiosity is the infancy of intelligence and the seed of knowledge. For today's journal entry, list four topics you are curious about, and four learning resources, to help satisfy your curiosities. Keep a copy of this list wherever you go. The next time you have a free moment, use your list to inspire self-motivated research. When you do this consistently, and with disciplined dedication, your small seeds of curiosity will eventually grow into tall trees of knowledge.

Date: ____/____/____

List four topics you are curious about (As) and four learning resources to help satisfy your curiosities (Bs).

1A)_____

2A)_____

3A)_____

4A)_____

1B)_____

2B)_____

3B)_____

4B)_____

Extra Expressings and Thoughtful Thinkings: On the lines below, choose a never before done activity/hobby. Do it for four days and write about it.

_____

_____

_____

_____

_____

_____

"The most beautiful thing we can experience is the mysterious. He to whom this emotion is a stranger, who can no longer pause to wonder and stand rapt in awe, is as good as dead; his eyes are closed." ~ Albert Einstein

Think your morning JUICE. There's a line from the movie *Shakespeare in Love*. The character is talking about how theater production problems seem to magically solve themselves at the last minute. He's asked, "How will it work?" He replies, "I don't know. It's a mystery." For today's journal entry, list a few situations you see as one of life's magical mysteries. Who knows, maybe someday you'll be the one to discover their solutions. Then read the quote and describe your inspired thoughts and feelings.

Date: _____/_____/_____

List of a few situations you see as one of life's magical mysteries. Why?

1) _____

_____

2) _____

_____

3) _____

_____

4) _____

_____

Read the quote and describe your inspired thoughts and feelings.

_____

_____

_____

_____

"Disciplined activity and heightened sensitivity can reveal a spiritual path for the artist, which can lead to a private spring of magical waters." ~ Richard Newman

Think your morning JUICE. For today's journal entry, list a couple "disciplined activities." Explain how your unique interests help. For example, I make jewelry. This healthy habit/hobby is analogous to adult Legos. It helps my life because it provides me with a fun outlet for creative energy, and I am able to make special occasions personalized, and pretty gifts for my friends and family.

Date: ____/____/____

List a couple disciplined activities.

1) _____

_____

2) _____

_____

Explain how these activities help.

1) _____

_____

_____

_____

2) _____

_____

_____

_____

"The spiritual is not something that descends from above, rather it is an illumination that is to be discovered within." ~ Ajit Mookerjee

Think your morning JUICE. That is why they call it, "en-(in)-light-enment." For today's journal entry, read the quote, look at the photographs below, and describe your inspired thoughts and feelings.

Date: ____ / ____ / ____

Describe your inspired thoughts on enlightenment.

_____

_____

_____

_____

"My religion is loving-kindness." ~ The Dalai Lama (Answering "What is your religion?")

Think your morning JUICE. I love this quote. It's a unique and beautiful answer to a very common question. Wouldn't it be wonderful if everyone on Earth could answer how the foundation of their religion is, "loving kindness"? For today's journal entry, read the quote, describe your inspired thoughts and feelings, and write your answer to the quote's question. Don't simply describe your religion's labels or use the dogma words which you've heard and learned from external sources. Openly describe how you feel inside. Write about what you truly believe. As best you can, clearly explain the foundation of your faith.

Date: ____/____/____

Read the quote and describe your inspired thoughts and feelings.

_____

_____

_____

_____

Write your answer to the quote's question and, as best you can, clearly explain the foundation of your faith.

_____

_____

_____

_____

Exercise 2 - PIES: A Four-Part Character Study

Think your morning JUICE. Use this page to continue, or redo Exercise 1. Then, when you have completed the exercise, describe your inspired thoughts and feelings.

Date: ____/____/____

_____

_____

_____

_____

_____

_____

_____

_____

_____

_____

_____

Part Three: The Holistic Life Resumé

"Let us dare to be ourselves, for we can do that better than anyone." ~ Shirley Briggs

Think your morning JUICE. This quote perfectly parallels the concept of being A Perfect You. It reminds us how we are the only people who can best be ourselves. So by all means dare to be you. For today's journal entry, read the quote, consider the concept, and describe your inspired thoughts and feelings. Answer the question, "How does thinking of yourself in this way help you deal with your personal, external self-image, and internal self-esteem concerns?"

Date: _____/_____/_____

Read the quote, consider the concept, and describe your inspired thoughts and feelings.

_____

_____

_____

_____

Answer the writing prompt question.

_____

_____

_____

_____

"Since you're like no other being ever created, … you're incomparable." ~ Brenda Ueland

Think your morning JUICE. Continue writing on the Perfect You concept. Write about a couple incomparable people, characters you know. Explain why you see them this way. Describe how you are incomparable. Elaborate on a couple key points from your Holistic Life Resumé. And finally, write about an incomparable animal character in your family.

Date: _____/_____/_____

Write about a couple incomparable people, characters you know. Explain why you see them this way.

1) _____

_____

2) _____

_____

Describe how you are incomparable.

_____

_____

_____

_____

_____

_____

Elaborate on a couple key points from your Holistic Life Resumé.

1) _____

_____

2) _____

_____

And finally, write about an incomparable animal character in your family.

Name:_____

_____

_____

_____

_____

_____

_____

Extra Expressings and Thoughtful Thinkings: On the lines below, give names and short captions for these four incomparable characters.

1) _____

_____

2) _____

_____

3) _____

_____

4) _____

_____

Presentize Yourself!

Andrewism: The Mirror's Reply

I Look,   At The Mirror.
I See,   The Image It Reflects.
I Wonder,   "What Do Others See?"
I Wonder,   "What Do Others Think?"
I Wonder,   "What Do I See?"
I Wonder,   "What Do I Think?"
I Ask Myself,   "Do I Like My Mirror Image?"
I Ask Myself,   "Do I Like Myself?"
The Mirror's Reply: "You Is You.
                    Me Is Me.
                    Nothing, Nor No One, Can Take That Away From Either Of Us.
                    Please,
                    On The Outside And On The Inside,
                    Be The Very Best Person You Can Be.
                    Then, Most Importantly, For Both Our Sakes,
                    Be Yourself. And Always Remember, "You Are A Perfect You!""

I Have Answered My Questions In Silence.
I Have Answered Soundly.

Think your morning JUICE. This *Andrewism* poetry piece is my morning, mirror-time mantra. It's been very helpful in my life's trials and tribulations, and it's one of several tools I use to presentize myself. With this poetry piece, I remind myself of the previous section's Perfect You concept. For today's journal entry, take a good, long look at yourself in a full-length mirror. Read the poetry piece aloud. Hear the words. Listen with your heart. Describe your inspired thoughts and feelings. And if you want, write your own poetry piece.

Date: _____/_____/_____

Read the *Andrewism* poetry piece aloud and describe your inspired thoughts and feelings.

_____

_____

_____

_____

_____

_____

If you want, write your own poetry piece.

Title:_____

_____

_____

_____

_____

_____

_____

_____

_____

_____

_____

_____

_____

Andrewism: Who I Am Now!

Who Am I?	My Name Is Andrew S. Taylor	
I Know,	Who I Was.	
I Was,	Planning For,	"The Future," To Become, "The Now."
I Know,	Now,	"The Future," Never, "Presents" Itself, As, "The Now."
"The Past,"	Is A Memory.	
"The Future,"	Is A May-Be.	
"The Present,"	Is All That Ever Is.	
Who Am I,	Now?	
I Am Who I Am,	Now.	
I Am Who I Am,	Right Now, Within This One, Singular, Sensational, Solitary, Magical, Moment.	
I Am,	My Life,	Now!

Think your morning JUICE. This *Andrewism* poetry piece, is another tool I use to presentize myself. I read it, and I remember how all we really have in life is, "This One, Singular, Sensational, Solitary, Magical, Moment." For today's journal entry, read the poetry piece, describe your inspired thoughts and feelings, and list a few tools you use to presentize yourself. Finally, if you want, write your own, "Who I Am Now" poetry piece. Remember we established how poetry doesn't have to rhyme or follow any, "standard rules" of format or structure. So be as creative as you want. The bottom line is: Writing poetry is supposed to be fun. Have fun!

Date: ____/____/____

Read the poetry piece and describe your inspired thoughts and feelings.

_____

_____

_____

_____

List a few tools you use to presentize yourself.

1) _____

_____

2) _____

_____

3) _____

_____

4) _____

_____

Finally, if you want, write your own "Who I Am Now" poetry piece.

Title:_____

_____

_____

_____

_____

_____

_____

_____

_____

_____

_____

_____

_____

_____

"To love oneself, is the beginning of a lifelong romance." ~ Oscar Wilde

Think your morning JUICE. There's a commonly held belief; you can't love anybody until you can love yourself. So, why not get started? Appreciate all your good qualities and begin your "lifelong romance." For today's journal entry, read the quote, consider the concept, and describe your inspired thoughts and feelings.

Date: ____/____/____

Read the quote, consider the concept, and describe your inspired thoughts and feelings.

_____

_____

_____

_____

"Love yourself first and everything else will fall into place." ~ Lucille Ball

Think your morning JUICE. For today's journal entry, read the quote, consider the concept, and continue to describe your inspired thoughts and feelings. And know this noteworthy notion: When you're abundantly able to love yourself first, "everything else will fall into place."

Date: ____/____/____

Read the quote, consider the concept, and describe your inspired thoughts and feelings.

_____

_____

_____

_____

_____

_____

"If you are your own best friend, you will take delight in privacy. Whereas if you have no virtue or any self-noteworthy abilities, then you will be your own worst enemy and you will be afraid of solitude." ~ Aristotle

Think your morning JUICE. Aristotle is suggesting two possibilities for how to live your life. You can be your best friend or your worst enemy. When you're the former, you'll like your own company. Otherwise, maybe not. I'm here to remind you to choose wisely! For today's journal entry, read the quote, make your choice, and describe your inspired thoughts and feelings.

Date: ____/____/____

Read the quote, make your choice, and describe your inspired thoughts and feelings.

_____

_____

_____

_____

_____

_____

Listen to the song "The Man in the Mirror" written by Siedah Garrett and Glen Ballard and sung by Michael Jackson.

Think your morning JUICE. This song has great lyrics. It parallels my *Andrewism* poetry piece "The Mirror's Reply." It explains how to presentize yourself, and it tells you what to do next. It says, if you want to achieve any real improvement for yourself and the world, you need to look at yourself in the mirror and choose to change. The irony here is that the pop singer who made this song lyric famous was Michael Jackson. When he looked in the mirror, he chose to make only physical changes. He might have had a plethora of intellectual, emotional, and spiritual qualities he could've worked on, but if he made those changes, it was not obvious to many of those watching his behavior. For today's journal entry, choose a few more personal items you want to change. Explain why and how you want to make these changes.

Date: ____/____/____

Choose a few more personal items you want to change.

1) _____   3) _____

2) _____   4) _____

Explain why and how you want make these changes.

1) _____

_____

_____

_____

2) _____

_____

_____

_____

3) _____

_____

_____

_____

4) _____

_____

_____

_____

"Wherever you are, be there!" ~ Ralph Waldo Emerson

Think your morning JUICE. Obviously, this is easier said than done. Estimate your percentages. How much time is your mind someplace else? How much time are you thinking in the moment? For today's journal entry, answer these questions, write your percentages, and consider a few ideas how you might improve your numbers.

Date: _____/_____/_____

How much of the time is your mind someplace else? _____%

How much of the time are you thinking in the moment? _____%

Write a few ideas on how you might improve your numbers.

1) _____

_____

2) _____

_____

3) _____

_____

4) _____

_____

"Love the moment, and the energy of the moment will spread beyond all boundaries."
~ Corita Kent

Think your morning JUICE. This is another, "live in the moment" quote. It reminds you to, "love the moment." For today's journal entry, read the quote and describe your inspired thoughts and feelings.

Date: _____/_____/_____

Read the quote and describe your inspired thoughts and feelings.

_____

_____

_____

_____

"Begin doing what you want to do now. We have only this moment, sparkling like a star in our hand, and melting like a snowflake." ~ Marie Beynon Ray

Think your morning JUICE. This quote presents a perfect piece of advice. It says, "Begin doing what you want to do now." So, choose what you want to do and Just Do It!" (Nike) Take the first step! For today's journal entry, list four of your best, life-changing actions and describe how you felt after they were amazingly accomplished.

Date: _____/_____/_____

List four of your best, life-changing actions.

1) _____
_____

2) _____
_____

3) _____
_____

4) _____
_____

Describe how you felt after your actions were amazingly accomplished.

1) _____
_____

2) _____
_____

3) _____
_____

4) _____
_____

"You may have a fresh start at any moment you choose, for the thing we call, 'failure,' is not falling down, but staying down." ~ Mary Pickford

Think your morning JUICE. This quote explains what it means to presentize yourself. Two questions it inspires are, "How has life knocked you down?" and "How did you get up after each fall?" And you need to know how every time you made the choice to get up, and you actually did it, you successfully created a fresh start. For today's journal entry, answer the two questions, review a recent experience of successfully getting up to presentize yourself, and describe your inspired thoughts and feelings.

Date: ____ / ____ / ____

How has life knocked you down? List four examples.

1) _____
   _____

2) _____
   _____

3) _____
   _____

4) _____
   _____

How did you get up after each fall?

1) _____
   _____
   _____
   _____

2) _____
   _____
   _____
   _____

3) _____
   _____
   _____
   _____

4) _____
   _____
   _____
   _____

(Noteworty Note: If you need/want more empowering examples of this quote's message, I'm sure you can find a vast variety, used by every athletic/sports coach who ever lived and desired to inspire success!)

Review a recent experience of successfully getting up to presentize yourself and describe your inspired thoughts and feelings.

_____

_____

_____

_____

Andrewism: The Time Is Now!

Live Your Day To It's Fullest.   This May Be Your Last Day.
     Sunrise, Dawn, High Noon, Dusk, & Sunset: These Are Just Moments In Time.
Life Is A Day.   What's The Motto With You?   Carpe' Diem.
          Yesterday, Yesteryear, Someday, & Sometime: These Are Nothing.
There Is Only Now.   What Time Is It?   The Time Is Now.

Think your morning JUICE. For today's journal entry, read the *Andrewism* poetry piece, and describe your inspired thoughts and feelings. Then write your new life philosophy and your own mental motto.

Date: ____/____/____

Read the *Andrewism* poetry piece, and describe your inspired thoughts and feelings.

_____

_____

_____

_____

Write your new, life philosophy.

_____

_____

_____

_____

Write your own, mental motto.

_____

_____

_____

_____

"One should count each day as a separate life." ~ Seneca

Think your morning JUICE. When I first read this quote I thought, "Yes. That sounds right, but only if you are also able to live with the mindset of Carpe Diem, seize the day!" What do you think of these two life philosophies being put together? For today's journal entry, read the quote, answer the writing prompt question, and describe your inspired thoughts and feelings.

Date: ____/____/____

Read the quote, answer the writing prompt question, and describe your inspired thoughts and feelings.

_____

_____

_____

_____

"No one can know where they're going, unless they know exactly where they've been, and exactly how they arrived at their present place." ~ Maya Angelou

Think your morning JUICE. This quote perfectly ends this section and segues into the next. In the first three sections, you plotted where you've been, and now you know exactly how you arrived at your present place. You were able to presentize yourself. In the next section, Find True (For You) North, you'll determine where you are going, but for today's journal entry, continue writing on any of the themes or ideas you've seen so far.

Date: _____/_____/_____

Continue writing on any of the themes or ideas you've seen so far.

_____

_____

_____

_____

Extra Expressings and Thoughtful Thinkings: On the lines below, ask yourself a few questions inspired by section titles soon to be seen.

Q:_____

_____

Q:_____

_____

Q:_____

_____

Q:_____

_____

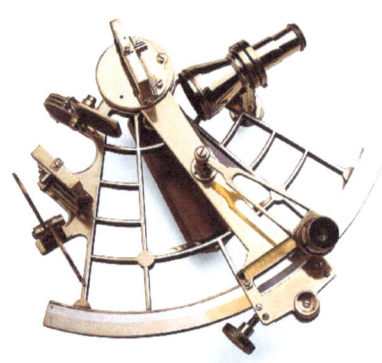

Find True (For You) North!

"No wind is true if you don't know the direction, or port, for which you are heading." ~ Seneca

"If you don't know where you are going, any road will get you there." ~ Lewis Carroll

Think your morning JUICE. With these two quotes in mind, determine your own direction. In the book I write, "I am a *teacher*, and my life philosophy is *harmony*." For today's journal entry, choose your own true north, life identity words. Then explain why you chose these specific words.

Date: ____/____/____

Choose your own true north, life identity words.

1) _____

_____

2) _____

_____

Explain why you chose theses specific words.

1) _____

_____

2) _____

_____

"You've got to be very careful. If you don't know where you're going you might not get there." ~ Yogi Berra

Think your morning JUICE. I've always like Yogi Berra quotes. They make you think, and at the same time, they put a smile on your face. For today's journal entry, read the quote, review the book section, and describe your inspired thoughts and feelings. Then write a few of your own unique and special, true north quotes.

Date: ____/____/____

Read the quote, review the book section, and describe your inspired thoughts and feelings.

_____

_____

_____

_____

Write a few of your own unique and special, true north quotes.

1) _____

_____

2) _____

_____

3) _____

_____

4) _____

_____

"One of the most courageous things you can do is identify yourself, know who you are, what you believe in and where you want to go." ~ Sheila Murray Bethel

Think your morning JUICE. Yes! Traveling on a journey of self-discovery is "one of the most courageous things you can do." You need to be congratulated for your efforts. You've done the work to identify yourself and you have a much better idea of "who you are, what you believe in, and where you want to go." You are now outstanding in your field of self-expertise. So, keep the momentum moving. Go on a solo, self-rewarding date. For today's journal entry, describe what you did on your date and explain how it rejuvenated your resolve to become a more self-improved person. Finally, write about any ambitious ideas and plans you may have for future dates.

Date: ____ / ____ / ____

Describe what you did on your date.

_____

_____

_____

_____

Explain how your date rejuvenated your resolve to become a more self-improved person.

_____

_____

_____

_____

Write about any ambitious ideas and plans you may have for future dates.

1) _____

_____

2) _____

_____

3) _____

_____

4) _____

_____

You are here!

(Use a, "you are here" dot to show how you are obviously outstanding in your field!)

"We're always free to go wherever we wish and to be whatever we are."
~ Johnathan Livingston Seagull as written by Richard Bach

Think your morning JUICE. Do you agree or disagree? Why? For today's journal entry, read the quote, answer the writing prompt question, and describe your inspired thoughts and feelings.

Date: ____/____/____

I agree____. I disagree____. Why?

_____

_____

_____

_____

(This is Jonathan Livingston Seagull, I presume!)

"Argue for your limitations and they're yours." ~ Richard Bach

Think your morning JUICE. As a teacher, I use this quote often with students who say, "I can't ..." I say, "Tell yourself you can and try again." This quote also applies to the previous inspiration and prompt. For those of you who made the argument of how we are not "free to go wherever we want and to be whatever we are," please rethink your original position. Then, whenever internal or external forces tell you "You can't ... ," simply tell yourself "I believe I can and I am free to try again." For today's journal entry, apply this thought transposing process to a couple of everyday situations and record your results.

Date: _____ / _____ / _____

First, write about the old situation.

1) _____

_____

2) _____

_____

Second, explain how you were able to rethink the old situations.

1) _____
_____
_____
_____

2) _____
_____
_____
_____

A) Third, write about the new situations.

B) Finally, record your results and describe your thoughts and feelings.

1A)_____
_____
_____

1B)_____
_____
_____

2A)_____
_____
_____

2B)_____
_____
_____

"Dream deep and reach high for the stars. For every dream precedes a goal."
~ Pamela Vaull Starr

Think your morning JUICE. To find your true (for you) north you need to truly dream deep. So once again, take this opportunity to divinely daydream. Yes, this is a workbook which enthusiastically encourages you to daydream! For today's journal entry, describe a couple more favorite daydreams and life ambitions. Then write three steps, (A, B, and C), you'll need to take before you can successfully accomplish your new goals.

Date: ____/____/____

Describe a couple more favorite daydreams and life ambitions.

1) _____

_____

2) _____

_____

Write three steps, (A, B, and C), you'll need to take before you can successfully accomplish your new goals.

1A)_____

_____

_____

_____

1B)_____

_____

_____

_____

1C)_____

_____

_____

_____

2A)_____

_____

_____

_____

2B)_____

_____

_____

_____

2C)_____

_____

_____

_____

Exercise 3 - True (For You) North Task Time

Think your morning JUICE. Use this page to continue or redo Exercise 3. Then, when you have completed the exercise, describe your inspired thoughts and feelings.

Date: ____/____/____

_____

_____

_____

_____

_____

_____

_____

_____

_____

_____

_____

_____

_____

_____

_____

_____

_____

_____

_____

_____

Set Sail!

"You are either the captive, or the captain, of your thoughts." ~ Denis Waitley

Think your morning JUICE. This quote presents you with a choice. Granted it seems like an easy choice, but it is a choice, nonetheless. For today's journal entry, make your choice and put it in writing. Then, after you've finished following this writing prompt, describe your inspired thoughts and feelings. Specifically describe how you believe your choice will manifest itself.

Date: _____ / _____ / _____

Make your choice and put it in writing. "I choose to be the _____ of my thoughts (captive or captain)." When you've successfully, and hopefully wisely, made your choice, describe your inspired thoughts and feelings.

_____

_____

_____

_____

Specifically describe how you believe your choice will manifest itself.

_____

_____

_____

_____

"Not I, nor anyone else, can travel the road for you. You must travel it for yourself."
~ Walt Whitman

Think your morning JUICE. Remember this is your life. You are the only one who can live it. So you be the one in the driver's seat and you be the captain of your ship. For today's journal entry, read the quote, look at the photographs below, and describe your inspired thoughts and feelings.

Date: ____/____/____

Read the quote, look at the photographs below, and describe your inspired thoughts and feelings.

_____

_____

_____

_____

_____

_____

"One does not discover new lands, without consenting to lose sight of the shore."
~ André Gide

Think your morning JUICE. Set sail! Discover the new you. In some small or grand way, make everyday a new life adventure. For today's journal entry, describe what you did today to successfully accomplish this goal. After a week, describe your inspired thoughts and feelings. Write about how you discovered new lands and made new life adventures.

Date: ____/____/____

Write about how you made Saturday a new life adventure.

_____

_____

Date: ____/____/____

Write about how you made Sunday a new life adventure.

_____

_____

Date: ____/____/____

Write about how you made Monday a new life adventure.

_____

_____

Date: ____/____/____

Write about how you made Tuesday a new life adventure.

_____

_____

Date: ____/____/____

Write about how you made Wednesday a new life adventure.

_____

_____

Date: _____/_____/_____

Write about how you made Thursday a new life adventure.

_____

_____

Date: _____/_____/_____

Write about how you made Friday a new life adventure.

_____

_____

Date: _____/_____/_____

Hello. It's Saturday again. So describe your inspired thoughts and feelings and write about your discovered new lands and your new life adventures. In short, write about your wonderful week.

_____

_____

_____

_____

"Dreams are the touchstones of our character." ~ Henry David Thoreau

Think your morning JUICE. Touchstones are equal to stepping-stones on a garden path. So once again, if you want a clue, as to who you are and where your character is on the path of life, simply take a look at your dreams. For today's journal entry, continue writing about your dreams and ambitions. Either write more about the ones you've already mentioned, or write your thoughts and feelings about a few new ones you've recently created.

Date: _____/_____/_____

Describe a few dreams and ambitions.

1) _____

_____

_____

_____

2) _____

_____

_____

_____

3) _____

_____

_____

_____

4) _____

_____

_____

_____

"Whatever you can dream about doing or whatever you can do right now, begin it! Boldness has genius, power, and magic in it!" ~ Johann Wolfgang Von Goethe

Think your morning JUICE. Think about your dreams and ambitions. List four steps you will take toward achieving them in reality. Then reread the first step and take action on it immediately. For today's journal entry, after you've accomplished the step, describe your inspired thoughts and feelings. Remember to be bold for, "Boldness has genius, power, and magic in it!"

Date: _____/_____/_____

List four steps you will take toward achieving your dreams and ambitions in reality.

1) _____

2) _____

3) _____

4) _____

Reread the first step and take action on it immediately. When you've accomplished the step, describe your inspired thoughts and feelings. Remember to be bold.

_____

_____

_____

_____

"Go confidently in the direction of your dreams! Live the life you've imagined."
~ Henry David Thoreau

Think your morning JUICE. During one of my presentations, I divided an audience of teenagers into two small groups of males and females. I wanted them to have a candid conversation about, "What is the most attractive internal character trait?" It was unanimous! Confidence was number one! For today's journal entry, answer the question, "Do you agree or disagree that confidence is the most attractive internal character trait?" If you disagree, which character trait do you think is the most attractive and why? If you agree, explain why? Personally, I agree. Confidence is number one!

Date: _____/_____/_____

I disagree_____. I think _____ is the most attractive internal character trait.

I agree_____.

I think this way because:

_____

_____

_____

_____

"The method of the enterprising is to plan with audacity; to execute with vigor; to create a map of possibilities; and then to treat them all as probabilities." ~ Bovee

Think your morning JUICE. I like how this quote uses the word "audacity." Usually, this word has a negative connotation. But here, it's used positively. I also like how this quote upgrades possibilities to probabilities. This is a much better way to think. For today's journal entry, list a few possibilities you would like to think of as probabilities. Then when your list is finished, and you've transposed your new thinking, describe your inspired thoughts and feelings.

Date: ____/____/____

List of a few possibilities you'd like to think of as probabilities.

1) _____

_____

2) _____

_____

3) _____

_____

4) _____

_____

When your list is finished, and you've transposed your new thinking, describe your inspired thoughts and feelings.

_____

_____

_____

_____

"Positive thinking is useless unless it promotes positive action." ~ Dr. Robert Anthony

Think your morning JUICE. This quote is totally true and it's a great reminder. As you read the book and complete this workbook, remember it's all practically pointless if you don't put what you read and write into practice. In short, use it or lose it. For today's journal entry, write about a couple of the positive thoughts and ideas you've recorded in this book and describe how you are productively applying them in your daily life. Think of this as a good opportunity to document your successful self-improvement.

Date: ____/____/____

Write about a couple positive thoughts and ideas you've recorded in this book and describe how you are productively applying them in your daily life.

1) _____

_____

_____

_____

2) _____

_____

_____

_____

"An ounce of action is worth a ton of theory." ~ Friedrich Engels

Think your morning JUICE. This next section focuses on creative visualization and making a Projected Life Plan. But once again, all the mental imagery and projected life planning in the world is still practically pointless if you don't put it into practice and take action. For today's journal entry, write about a few external examples.

Date: _____/_____/_____

Choose four incredible inventions, which if action had never been taken and they were abandoned all together as un-inspirational ideas, our world would be a very different place.

1) _____

2) _____

3) _____

4) _____

Explain why you chose these individual items.

1) _____

_____

2) _____

_____

3) _____

_____

4) _____

   _____

"Follow your bliss! Put yourself on the right track. Commit yourself to your bliss and doors will open for you where there were no doors before and where there would not be any doors, open for anyone else." ~ Joseph Campbell

Think your morning JUICE. For today's journal entry, follow Joseph Campbell's amazing advice and describe your inspired thoughts and feelings. Also write about how some special, life-opportunity doors opened specifically and especially for you.

Date: ____/____/____

Follow the quote's amazing advice and describe your inspired thoughts and feelings.

_____

_____

_____

_____

_____

_____

_____

Write about how some special, life-opportunity doors opened specifically and especially for you.

_____

_____

_____

_____

_____

_____

_____

_____

Even if you're on the right track, if you just sit still, you will still get run over by the train."
~ Will Rogers

Think your morning JUICE. The previous page's Joseph Campbell quote said, "Put yourself on the right track." This Will Rogers' quote restates the point, how you can't just sit still on the right track. You also need to take immediate action. For today's journal entry, explain why it's so important to take immediate action.

Date: ____/____/____

Explain why it's so important to take immediate action.

_____

_____

_____

_____

_____

_____

"You can't make footprints in the sands of time by sitting on your butt. And besides, who wants to leave butt prints in the sands of time?" ~ Bob Moawad

Think your morning JUICE. This is a great quote. It's a funny and clever way to remind you to get off your butt and keep taking immediate action toward reaching your dreams. For today's journal entry, keep writing on this concept. Then tell a friend about it and describe what it feels like to (as the movie says) *Pay It Forward!*

Date: ____/____/____

Keep writing about why it's so important to take immediate action toward reaching your dreams.

_____

_____

_____

_____

Tell a friend what you've experienced and describe what it feels like to (as the movie says) *Pay It Forward!*

_____

_____

_____

_____

"Only those who risk going too far can possibly find out how far we can go." ~ T. S. Eliot

Think your morning JUICE. This quote parallels a previously mentioned André Gide quote. It is also a nice way to end the Set Sail! section. For today's journal entry, list a few risks you've taken and write about how they negatively held you back, or how they positively propelled your life forward.

Date: ____/____/____

List of a few risks you've taken.

1) _____

2) _____

3) _____

4) _____

Write about how these risks have negatively held you back or how they positively propelled your life forward.

1) _____

_____

_____

_____

2) _____

_____

_____

_____

3) _____

_____

_____

_____

4) _____

_____

_____

_____

Exercise 4 - Centering Yourself: A Three-Step Process

Think your morning JUICE. Use this page to continue or redo Exercise 4. Then, when you have completed the exercise, describe your inspired thoughts and feelings.

Date: ____/____/____

_____

_____

_____

_____

_____

_____

_____

_____

_____

_____

_____

_____

_____

_____

_____

_____

_____

_____

_____

_____

_____

Exercise 5 - Creative Visualization: Manifest Your Mental Imagery

Think your morning JUICE. Use this page to continue or redo Exercise 5. Then, when you have completed the exercise, describe your inspired thoughts and feelings.

Date: ____/____/____

_____

_____

_____

_____

_____

_____

_____

_____

_____

_____

_____

_____

_____

_____

_____

_____

_____

_____

_____

_____

Post View

"You must see all your goals clearly and specifically before you can confidently set out for them on your journey. Hold them in your mind until they become second nature." ~ Les Brown

"This is a time of great beginning. It is a time to die to who we used to be, to discover where we are at in this present moment, and to become who we are ultimately and uniquely capable of being. That is the gift that awaits us now: the chance to become who we really are, and to manifest our best self." ~ Marianne Williamson

Think your morning JUICE. When I first read these quotes, I knew they had to be in the workbook. I also knew they'd fit perfectly at the end of this chapter. For today's journal entry, continue writing about a few favorite concepts, read the quotes, and describe your inspired thoughts and feelings. Give each concept a reference title.

Date: ____ / ____ / ____

Continue writing about a few favorite concepts.

Concept Title 1)_____

_____

_____

_____

_____

_____

Concept Title 2) _____

_____

_____

_____

_____

_____

Concept Title 3) _____

_____

_____

_____

_____

_____

Concept Title 4) _____

_____

_____

_____

_____

_____

Read the quotes and describe your inspired thoughts and feelings.

Quote 1) _____

_____

_____

_____

_____

_____

Quote 2) _____

_____

_____

_____

_____

"Destiny is not a matter of chance; it is a matter of choice. It is not a thing to be waited for; it is a thing to be achieved." ~ William Jennings Bryan

Think your morning JUICE. This quote is the source for what I said to the girl in The Elite Example story. For today's journal entry, complete these three writing prompts. First, read the quote and presentation story and describe your inspired thoughts and feelings. Second, gather a group of friends, classmates, and/or peers, and perform the presentation's exercise. When it's over, talk about your experience and write a short set of summary statements for each participant. Third, review a few of your favorite concepts from the chapter and continue to describe your inspired thoughts and feelings. Then when all that's done, continue our journey in Chapter 2: Human Being vs. Human Doing!

Date: ____/____/____

Read the quote and presentation story and describe your inspired thoughts and feelings.

_____

_____

_____

_____

Write a short set of summary statements for each participant in the presentation exercise.

1) _____

_____

_____

_____

2) _____

_____

_____

_____

3) _____

_____

_____

_____

4) _____

_____

_____

_____

5) _____

_____

_____

_____

6) _____

_____

_____

_____

7) _____
_____
_____
_____

8) _____
_____
_____
_____

9) _____
_____
_____
_____

10) _____
_____
_____
_____

11) _____
_____
_____
_____

12) _____
_____
_____
_____

13) _____
_____
_____
_____

14) _____

_____

_____

_____

15) _____

_____

_____

_____

16) _____

_____

_____

_____

17) _____

_____

_____

_____

18) _____

_____

_____

_____

19) _____

_____

_____

_____

20) _____

_____

_____

_____

Review a few favorite chapter concepts and continue to describe your inspired thoughts and feelings.

1) _____

_____

_____

_____

2) _____

_____

_____

_____

3) _____

_____

_____

_____

4) _____

_____

_____

_____

Extra Expressings and Thoughtful Thinkings: This is the end of Chapter 1: Character Crystallization! On the last (writing) lines of this chapter, express your thoughts on the natural wonders of the world! (Not just the seven official ones.) Describe any you've been to and seen with your own eyes. Make recommendations of places for others to visit. Make lists of places you want to go to in the future. Create plans. And finally, write a bit about how you now know *YOU* are an ultimately unique, notably nurtured, originally natural, wonderful wonder of the world!

Crystal Cave at Naica, Chihuahua, Mexico, one of the natural wonders of the world.

_____

_____

_____

_____

_____

_____

_____

_____

Extra Expressings and Thoughtful Thinkings: Positivity Paragraphs!

Dramatically DO & Live Your Life FANTASTIC!
Live life to its **F**ULL-est! With Passion & Purpose!
As it applies, always say, "Yes **A**ND ..." to/in life!
Live life as a **N**OVEL novelty! All new adventures!
Live your dreams! Do **T**HRIVING in an aliving!
Attitude Gratitude! **A**ND Anticipate Abundance!
Do your definition **S**UCCESSFUL! Live your truth!
Be& Do! Confidence & Commitment! **T**OTALLY!
In ALL life's important institutions ... GO ALL **I**N!
Let go what you can't! **C**ONTROL what you can!

Write your inspired thoughts and feelings.

_____
_____
_____
_____
_____
_____
_____
_____
_____
_____

YOUR LIFE'S QUINTESSENTIAL QUESTIONS:
Who Are You? The Unique-est Of All You-s! !
What Are You? Greater Than Sum All Parts!
Where Are You? The Precisely Perfect Place!
When Are You? The Presently Perfect Time!
Why Are You? TO BE & TO DO The Best You!
YOUR CHARACTER'S CODE OF CONDUCT IS:
LIVE YOUR LIFE! ! DO A PERFECT YOU! !
RETURN WORTHY ALL LOVE YOU'RE GIVEN!

Write your inspired thoughts and feelings.

_____
_____
_____
_____
_____
_____
_____
_____
_____
_____

You NEED:) To Be Told Today! You Are A(n):)
Abundance:) Perfection & Pricelessness!:)
Beautiful:) Beyond Belief! & I Believe In You!:)
Creative-ly:) Constructed Character! Unique!:)
Convergence:) Of Clever Conversations!:)
Defined:) By Divinity & Destiny!:) Your Path!:)
Empower-mental-able Entity:) & This Is True!:)
FANTASTIC:) Family Of Fun-Full-Facilitations!:)
EVERY DAY:) This Is What's KNEW! Do YOU!:)

Write your inspired thoughts and feelings.

_____
_____
_____
_____
_____
_____
_____
_____
_____

To whom it may, be beneficial to say,
"I believe, every pertinent person,
at one particular point in their life,
needs to hear, and subsequently to know,
their lives are of immeasurable value, their
future is a plethora of positive possibilities,
and they are lovable beyond all reason,
for all the right reasons!! So I say, in the eyes
of this beholder, this is all true for you!!"
THE MIRROR'S REPLY: I LOOK & I SEE ME!

Write your inspired thoughts and feelings.

_____
_____
_____
_____
_____
_____
_____
_____
_____
_____

MY-Qs: What Do OTHERS & I, See & Think?
Do I Like ME-MYSELF as I am in a mirror?
TM'sR: "You Is You! Me Is Me! NOTHING &
NO ONE, Can Take All This Away From US!
So Please! Outside & Inside! BE BEST YOU!
BE YOURSELF! YOU ARE A PERFECT YOU!
This real reply is graciously given in silence!
My mind's master message is seen as sound!

"I believe, every pertinent person,
at one particular point in their life,
needs to hear, and subsequently to know,
their lives are of immeasurable value, their
future is a plethora of positive possibilities,
and they are lovable beyond all reason,
for all the right reasons!! So I say, in the eyes
of this beholder, this is all true for you!!"

Presentize Yourself! NOW: The Greatest Gift!
The Past: Forgotten of not, it's forever gone!
The Future: Forcasted! Falsely OR Truly!
BUT FOR REALL-LY, IT DOES NOT MATTER!
Because factually, a future is a never to be!
So live in the moment! Center yourself in it!
Remember it is all well and wonderful to set
golden foals & strive for fame & fortune!...
But definitely do not do it, at the expense of
not dramatically doing, your ALIVING NOW!

There is MAGIC! You create it in your character!
Make Good Intelligent Choices! Do this every day!
Choices are the building blocks of our characters!
Little & Large! From foundation to tip top towers!
Life's Qs: Who, What, Where, When, & Why AM I?
& Every Day & MAGIC Moment: What do I want?
Life's A: The wonderful way to manifest MAGIC is
LIVE YOUR LIFE CONSCIOUSLY & CLEARLY! &
MAKE SURE ALL CHOICES ARE MADE BY YOU!

Write your inspired thoughts and feelings.
_____
_____
_____
_____
_____
_____
_____

Write your inspired thoughts and feelings.
_____
_____
_____
_____
_____
_____
_____
_____

Write your inspired thoughts and feelings.
_____
_____
_____
_____
_____
_____
_____
_____
_____

Write your inspired thoughts and feelings.
_____
_____
_____
_____
_____
_____
_____
_____

Okay. Take the next step. Turn the page.

CHAPTER 2:
HUMAN BEING VS. HUMAN DOING!

Preview

"Being is thoughtless. It Is beyond and beneath all categories of thought. Being is still. Expression, doing, this is the realization of creative thought. Doing is moving."
~ Author Unknown

Think your morning JUICE. This is a great quote to start Chapter 2, because it eloquently shows the difference between a Human Being and a Human Doing. For today's journal entry, continue doing the write thing. Write a few of your best creative thoughts, explain why you chose these particular examples, tell the story of the creative thoughts' origin.

Date: ____/____/____

Write a few of your best creative thoughts.

1) _____

2) _____

3) _____

4) _____

Explain why you chose these particular examples.

1) _____

2) _____

3) _____

4) _____

Tell the story of the creative thoughts' origin.

1) _____

_____

_____

_____

2) _____

_____

_____

_____

3) _____

_____

_____

_____

4) _____

_____

_____

_____

Coma vs. Conscious

"Synergy doesn't just happen. It's a process of traveling on a journey through a series of conscious choices." ~ Author Unknown

Think your morning JUICE. Choosing to read this book and work in this workbook is, "traveling on a journey." I encourage you to continue making more of these intelligent, conscious choices. This way synergistic synchronicities will continue to happily happen for you. For today's journal entry, write about a couple of these special life moments and describe your inspired thoughts and feelings.

Date: ____/____/____

Write about a couple synergistic synchronicities and describe your inspired thoughts and feelings.

1) _____

_____

_____

_____

2) _____

_____

_____

_____

"A discovery is an accident meeting a prepared mind." ~ Albert Szent-Gyorgyi

Think your morning JUICE. So be prepared! Be conscious and you will discover your most valuable possession. You will discover yourself. For today's journal entry, write about a couple of your most memorable, self-discovery moments. Describe how being conscious of your character traits helped you be a better, self-improved person.

Date: ____/____/____

Write about a couple of your most memorable, self-discovery moments.

1) _____

_____

2) _____

_____

Describe how being conscious of your character traits helped you be a better, self-improved person.

1) _____

_____

_____

_____

2) _____

_____

_____

_____

3) _____

_____

_____

_____

4) _____

_____

_____

_____

"Did you ever observe to whom the positive and productive accidents always happen? Chance only favors the prepared mind." ~ Louis Pasteur

Think your morning JUICE. Getting conscious is the key to being prepared. When you're conscious you believe in and become open to all the, "positive and productive," possibilities. For today's journal entry, write about a couple famous, serendipitous stories, which inspire you. Explain why you chose these particular stories and describe how the story inspires you.

Date: ____/____/____

Write about a couple famous, serendipitous stories, which inspire you on a daily basis. Explain why you chose these particular stories and describe how the story inspires you.

1) _____

_____

_____

_____

2) _____

_____

_____

_____

"Live life on purpose!" ~ Dolly Parton

Think your morning JUICE. This is to say, don't be the random result of coincidental chances. Instead, construct your character and live your life by making conscious choices.

For today's journal entry, write your thoughts and feelings on what living a conscious life means to you. Give a couple examples, how you apply this concept in your daily life.

Date: ____/____/____

Write your thoughts and feelings on what living a conscious life means to you.

_____

_____

_____

_____

Give a couple examples, how you apply this concept in your daily life.

1) _____

_____

_____

_____

2) _____

_____

_____

_____

Exercise 6 - Coma vs. Conscious: Clear Comparisons

Think your morning JUICE. Use this page to continue or redo Exercise 6. Then, when you have completed the exercise, describe your inspired thoughts and feelings.

Date: ____/____/____

_____

_____

_____

_____

_____

_____

_____

_____

_____

_____

_____

_____

_____

_____

_____

_____

_____

_____

Asleep vs. Awake

"When 'light bulb ideas' 'turn on' in your head, see them as 'bright ideas!'"
~ Andrew S. Taylor

Think your morning JUICE. Sometimes all it takes, is to think of one, great idea, and that's enough to wake a person up from their dispassionate, sleep walking existence. So use today's journal entry as if it's a proverbial paper napkin in a coffee shop. Describe a few of your best and brightest "Edisonesque" light bulb ideas.

Date: _____/_____/_____

Describe a few of your best and brightest "Edisonesque" light bulb ideas.

1) _____

_____

_____

_____

2) _____

_____

_____

_____

3) _____

_____

_____

_____

4) _____

_____

_____

_____

"May all beings everywhere be awakened, healed, peaceful, and free. May there be peace in this world and an end to war, poverty, violence, and oppression; and may we all, together, complete our spiritual journey." ~ Luma Surya Das

Think your morning JUICE. I do so sincerely hope, we all do so supremely share this quote's superbly splendid, sweet sentiment. For today's journal entry, read the quote, assert your agreement with it, and describe your inspired thoughts and feelings.

Date: ____/____/____

Read the quote, assert your agreement with it, and describe your inspired thoughts and feelings.

_____

_____

_____

_____

_____

_____

_____

_____

_____

_____

_____

_____

Aware vs. Alive

"Every decision you make and every action you take is based on your present level of awareness." ~ Dr. Robert Anthony

Think your morning JUICE. It stands to reason if you raise your level of awareness, you will improve the productivity of your decisions, and your actions will produce more positive results. For today's journal entry, read the quote and describe your inspired thoughts and feelings. Then, describe a couple examples, which display your new level of awareness.

Date: _____/_____/_____

Read the quote and describe your inspired thoughts and feelings.

_____

_____

_____

_____

Describe a couple examples, which display your new level of awareness.

1) _____

_____

_____

_____

2) _____

_____

_____

_____

"I think what we're seeking is an experience of being alive! So our life experience, on the purely physical plane, will have a resonance within our own innermost soul, so we actually feel the rapture of being alive!" ~ Joseph Campbell

"We can only be said to be alive, in those moments, when our hearts are conscious of our treasures." ~ Thorton Wilder

Think your morning JUICE. These quotes define this section. The first states how everyone who is aware is seeking an experience where they will "actually feel the rapture of being alive." The second defines what it means to be alive. For today's journal entry, read the quotes and describe your inspired thoughts and feelings. Then, write about a few moments when you've felt totally alive, and tell how these experiences changed your life.

Date: ____/____/____

Read the quotes and describe your inspired thoughts and feelings.

Quote 1) _____

_____

_____

_____

Quote 2) _____

_____

_____

_____

Write about a few moments when you've felt totally alive and tell how these experiences changed your life.

1) _____

_____

_____

_____

2) _____

_____

_____

_____

3) _____

_____

_____

_____

4) _____

_____

_____

_____

"Here's a test to find whether or not your mission on Earth is finished: If you're alive it isn't." ~ Richard Bach

Think your morning JUICE. I like to add to this that once you check your pulse, it also helps to have the amazing ability to *feel* absolutely alive. For today's journal entry, answer the question, "What do you think are four, key ingredients or character traits, which help you feel totally alive?" Explain your choices.

Date: ____/____/____

List the key ingredients or character traits, which help you feel totally alive and explain your choices.

1) _____

_____

_____

_____

2) _____

_____

_____

_____

3) _____

_____

_____

_____

4) _____

_____

_____

_____

"All men die, few men live." ~ Mel Gibson as William Wallace

Think your morning JUICE. Now you are aware of this quote from *Braveheart*. So make a promise. Say, "I will completely live my life. I will be totally alive!" For today's journal entry, list a few actions you will take to ensure that you will keep your promise.

Date: _____ / _____ / _____

List a few actions you will take to ensure that you will keep your promise.

1) _____

2) _____

3) _____

4) _____

"Strive to be holistically alive and you will whole heartedly thrive!" ~ Andrew S. Taylor

Think your morning JUICE. You've written about moments when you've felt totally and completely alive. Now write about a few favorite external examples? For today's journal entry, list a few favorite members of your Triple AAA (Admirable And Alive) club. Explain why you chose these particular people and describe how they inspire you.

Date: _____/_____/_____

List a few favorite Triple AAA Members.

1) _____

2) _____

3) _____

4) _____

Explain why you chose these particular people and describe how they inspire you.

1) _____

_____

_____

_____

2) _____

_____

_____

_____

3) _____

_____

_____

_____

4) _____

_____

_____

_____

Mind-Full vs. Mind-Free

"Universal consciousness intuition… this is the origin of all art." ~ Piet Mondrian

Think your morning JUICE. For today's journal entry, (A) describe how "universal conscious-ness intuition" influences you. (B) List a few of your mind-full technical skills or artistic proficiencies. (C) Finally, describe how it feels to perform these activities in a mind-free state.

Date: ____ / ____ / ____

A) _____

_____

_____

_____

_____

_____

B)

1) _____

2) _____

3) _____

4) _____

C)

1) _____

_____

2) _____

_____

3) _____

_____

4) _____

_____

  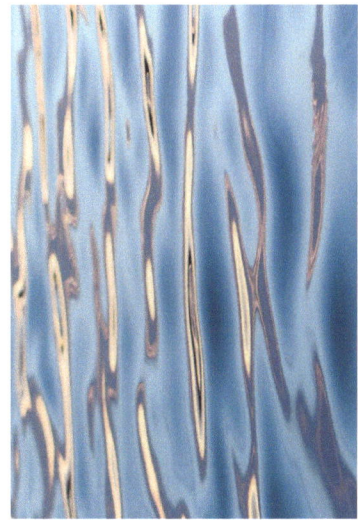

"Inspiration may be a form of super-consciousness, or perhaps sub-consciousness - I wouldn't know. But I am sure it is the antithesis of self-consciousness." ~ Aaron Copland

Think your morning JUICE. I like this quote for two reasons. One, Copland says, "I don't know." I like it when an assumed expert admits to this pervasive condition. And two, it states how inspiration (doing mind-free actions and activities) is the antithesis of self-consciousness (or being mind-full). For fun, write a few thoughts on a subject you admit to knowing nothing about. Perhaps you will inspire a new, healthy curiosity. Then read the quote and describe your inspired thoughts and feelings.

Date: _____ / _____ / _____

Write a few thoughts on a subject you admit to knowing nothing about.

_____

_____

_____

_____

Read the quote and describe your inspired thoughts and feelings.

_____

_____

_____

_____

"No longer conscious of my movement, I discovered a new unity with nature. I had found a new source of power and beauty, a source I never dreamt even existed." ~ Roger Bannister

(His thoughts on being the first person to break the four-minute mile.)

Think your morning JUICE. Clearly this was a mind-free moment in human history. Since you've already written about some of your own mind-free actions, activities, and moments, list a few examples you've seen performed by other people. Explain why you chose these particular moments and describe how they inspired you.

Date: _____/_____/_____

List a few examples of mind-free moments you've seen performed by other people.

1) _____

2) _____

3) _____

4) _____

Explain why you chose these particular moments and describe how they inspired you.

1) _____

_____

2) _____

_____

3) _____

_____

4) _____

_____

"When one is engaged in a favorite pursuit or a subject, absorbingly interesting, the normal conception of labor or time and artificial social distinctions disappear from the mind. In fact, life itself is absorbed in the engagement, or it may be said that one's life is tuned in harmony with all eternal life." ~ G. Koizumi

Think your morning JUICE. In short: Time flies when you're having fun! This is one of the best side effects of acting in a mind-free state. And since you've already written about mind-free activities, which you and other people have done, for today's journal entry, list of a few activities, which you've recently learned about, and which you'd like to do in the near future. Write about how and when you will do these mind-free activities.

Date: _____/_____/_____

List of a few activities which you've recently learned about and you'd like to do in the near future.

1) _____

2) _____

3) _____

4) _____

Write about how and when you will do these mind-free activities.

1) _____

2) _____

3) _____

4) _____

Andrewism: Please Promise Me Patrick!

From: Andrew S. Taylor 12/16/1968 - _____/_____/_____
            Dear Best Friend & Brother,
                  I Will Remember You For The Rest Of My Life.
                  I Knew You For 20 Years.
                  I Will Love You For The Rest Of My Life.
                  Today, "The Rest Is Silence."
To: PATRICK J. SWENSON 8/8/1969 - 8/1/1998
To: All Who Love (&) To: All Who Are Loved By Others: Please Promise Me! USE SEAT BELTS!

Think your morning JUICE. This *Andrewism* poetry piece, was my literary response to Patrick's death. Please share it with your family and friends and if it's necessary, hopefully they will make you a promise to always use seat belts. For today's journal entry, read the *Andrewism* poetry piece, and describe your inspired thoughts and feelings. Then, write about your experience of sharing it with family and friends. If you want, or feel the need, write your own poetry piece which matches the sentiment.

Date: ____/____/____

Read the *Andrewism* poetry piece, and describe your inspired thoughts and feelings.

_____

_____

_____

_____

_____

Write about your experiences of sharing it with family and friends.

_____

_____

_____

_____

_____

If you want, or feel the need, write your own poetry piece, which matches the sentiment.

Title:_____

_____

_____

_____

_____

_____

_____

_____

_____

_____

_____

_____

Exercise 7 - Stage Review: Where are You in The Planet's Population

Think your morning JUICE. Use this page to continue or redo Exercise 7. Then, when you have completed the exercise, describe your inspired thoughts and feelings.

Date: ____/____/____

_____

_____

_____

_____

_____

_____

_____

_____

_____

_____

_____

_____

_____

Focus and Pay Attention!

"You can observe a lot by watching." ~ Yogi Berra

Think your morning JUICE. I love Yogi Berra quotes. With his comic commentary, he always presents a meaningful and subtle truth. For today's journal entry, answer the following question, "What, or who, do you observe and watch the most?" List a few choices and explain why you find these subjects so entertaining. Then, answer the prompting questions, which refer to the photograph shown on the following page.

Date: _____/_____/_____

What, or who, do you observe and watch the most? List a few choices. Explain why.

1) _____

_____

2) _____

_____

3) _____

_____

4) _____

_____

Explain why you find these subjects so entertaining.

1) _____

_____

2) _____

_____

3) _____

_____

4) _____

_____

Look at the photograph on the following page. What, or who, do you think this beautiful bird is focusing on and paying attention to? What do you think is going to happen next?

Question 1) _____

_____

Question 2) _____

_____

"When you stay focused and keep your commitments you create momentum. And momentum begets momentum." ~ Rich Fettke

Think your morning JUICE. The key words in this quote are "keep your commitments." This is paramount to producing a positive self-character. You need to keep all your promises. Even - and especially - the silent ones you make with yourself. The bottom-line truth: Don't make a promise you can't keep! For today's journal entry, read the quote and describe your inspired thoughts and feelings.

Date: _____/_____/_____

Read the quote and describe your inspired thoughts and feelings.

_____

_____

_____

_____

"You can't depend on your judgment when your imagination is out of focus." ~ Mark Twain

Think your morning JUICE. This quote sets an interesting paradox within an unusually different paradigm. Most people seem to think our imagination is separate from our judgment of reality. But this quote makes the argument that they must work together to function properly, and your ability to focus is a fundamental factor for both. Do you agree or disagree? For today's journal entry, read the quote and describe your inspired thoughts and feelings. Then answer the question and explain your answer.

Date: ____/____/____

Read the quote and describe your inspired thoughts and feelings.

_____

_____

_____

_____

Answer the question: I agree_____ or I disagree_____ and explain why.

_____

_____

_____

_____

"Put all your eggs in one basket and watch that basket!" ~ Mark Twain

Think your morning JUICE. This is another great quote by Mark Twain. I include it here, (instead of in Chapter 4 where it appears in the book,) for two reasons. First, it's a wonderful example of how you need to focus and pay attention. Second, it shows how two pieces of guru-given advice, on the same subject, can have entirely different, and yet equally valid, points of view. One guru says you need to diversify, be cautious, put all your eggs in several baskets: Focus on The Big Picture. And another guru says, you need to consolidate, "Put all your eggs in one basket," and very carefully "watch that basket!" Focus on The Small Picture. My point is you need to focus by whichever method works best for you! And either way, you need to pay attention! For today's journal entry, read the quote, consider all the points, and describe your inspired thoughts and feelings.

Date: ____/____/____

Read the quote, consider all the points, and describe your inspired thoughts and feelings.

_____

_____

_____

_____

"Courage is the price life exacts for granting peace." ~ Amelia Earhart

Think your morning JUICE. This quote helps me illustrate the difference between potential energy and kinetic energy. It also helps me talk about current-cy, (in the now) energy. The quote implies how when you are courageous; you are able to focus and transform your negative, inhibiting energy into positive, productive energy. For today's journal entry, read the quote and describe your inspired thoughts and feelings. Then write about a time when you were courageous. Explain how, as a result, life granted you peace.

Date: _____/_____/_____

Read the quote and describe your inspired thoughts and feelings.

_____

_____

_____

_____

Write about a time when you were courageous. Explain how, as a result, life granted you peace.

_____

_____

_____

_____

"You have to pay close attention to what you love, and never listen to anyone who tells you to be practical too early on in the game." ~ Barbara Sher

Think your morning JUICE. Has anyone ever proposed you need to be more practical? For today's journal entry, do the following writing prompt. If your answer is "Yes," write about a time when this happened and describe your response. If your answer is "No," write about how you'd respond if this did happen to you.

Date: _____/_____/_____

Yes_____ or No_____

Describe your response.

_____

_____

_____

_____

"The actual cost of a thing is the amount of what I call life, which is required to be exchanged for it, immediately or in the long run." ~ Henry David Thoreau

Think your morning JUICE. For today's journal entry, list up to twelve of your most valuable acquisitions and/or possessions. Determine each item's value by how much focus and attention time it took to obtain. This is how much current-cy, (in-the-now) energy, you had to, "pay!" (Note: You don't need to limit your answers to only material items. You can list an academic degree, an occupational title, a friend, a spouse, a child, or anything, which is highly valuable to you.)

Date: _____/_____/_____

List up to twelve of your most valuable acquisitions and/or possessions.

1) _____

2) _____

3) _____

4) _____

5) _____

6) _____

7) _____

8) _____

9) _____

10) _____

11) _____

12) _____

Describe how much focus and attention time it took for you to obtain each item.

1) _____

2) _____

3) _____

4) _____

5) _____

6) _____

7) _____

8) _____

9) _____

10) _____

11) _____

12) _____

"What holds attention, determines actions." ~ William James

Think your morning JUICE. For today's journal entry, answer the question, "If you were a professional photographer what would be your top two, favorite subjects?" Recognize how these subject choices hold your attention and determine your actions. Write about why you'd choose these particular subjects and list a few actions you'd do to be more involved with your subjects. For example, Carole Fletcher is the fantastic photographer for this workbook. Her focus and attention is held by nature. So she became a professional photographer to spend more time outside.

Date: _____/_____/_____

If you were a professional photographer what would be your top two favorite subjects?

1) _____

_____

2) _____

_____

Write about why you'd choose these particular subjects.

1) _____

_____

_____

_____

2) _____

_____

_____

_____

List of a few actions you'd do, to be more involved with your subjects.

Subject 1)

1) _____

2) _____

3) _____

4) _____

Subject 2)

1) _____

2) _____

3) _____

4) _____

Exercise 8 - Four Focus Factors (FFs) and Their Corresponding Enhance Concentration Technique (ECTs)

Think your morning JUICE. Use this page to continue or redo Exercise 8. Then, when you have completed the exercise, describe your inspired thoughts and feelings. Pictures' Posts: And if you want to write about the four pictures, use the last four lines.

Date: ____/____/____

_____

_____

_____

_____

_____

_____

_____

_____

_____

_____

_____

_____

_____

_____

_____

_____

Pictures' Posts:

1) _____

2) _____

3) _____

4) _____

Help: Earn It!

"All you need to do to receive guidance, is ask for it, and then listen." ~ Sanaya Roman

Think your morning JUICE. The subsequent point of this quote is it doesn't matter whether you ask for and receive guidance in a formal (conscious) or informal (unconscious) way. What does matter, is even if you hear the most priceless piece of advice ever given, it is practically pointless if you don't also heed the advice. For today's journal entry, quote the best pieces of advice you've ever heard. Explain who, what, where, when, and how for each event. Then describe how heeding the advice has helped improve your life.

Date: ____/____/____

Quote the best pieces of advice you've ever heard. Explain who, what, where, when, and how, for each event.

Advice 1) _____

Event Explanation 1) _____

_____

_____

_____

Advice 2) _____

Event Explanation 2) _____

_____

_____

_____

Advice 3) _____

Event Explanation 3) _____

_____

_____

_____

Advice 4) _____

Event Explanation 4) _____

_____

_____

_____

Describe how heeding the advice has helped improve your life.

1) _____

_____

_____

_____

2) _____

_____

_____

_____

3) _____

_____

4) _____

_____

_____

_____

"Many things are lost for want of asking." ~ English Proverb

Think your morning JUICE. This proverb reminds me of a classical bit of dramatic dialogue. It usually sounds something like this: Guy to Girl: "Why didn't you tell me you liked me?" Girl to Guy: "You didn't ask." (Granted she didn't simply take the initiative and communicate to him how she felt either, but that's a journal entry for another day.) For today's journal entry, write about a couple questions you've been procrastinating about asking. Then actually ask your questions until you get acceptable answers. Write about your Q&A experience and your results.

Date: _____/_____/_____

Write about a couple, important questions you've been procrastinating about asking.

1) _____

_____

2) _____

_____

Write about your Q&A experience and your results.

1) _____

_____

_____

_____

2) _____

_____

_____

_____

"The vocation of every man and woman is to serve other people." ~ Leo Tolstoy

Think your morning JUICE. For today's journal entry, read the quote and describe your inspired thoughts and feelings. Then write about a couple ways you serve others, how you are served, and how you would like to serve others in the future. Explain why you have these desires and list an immediate action you can take toward accomplishing your goals.

Date: ____/____/____

Read the quote and describe your inspired thoughts and feelings.

_____

_____

_____

_____

Write about a couple ways you serve others.

1) _____

_____

2) _____

_____

Write about a couple ways you are served.

1) _____

_____

2) _____

_____

Write about a couple ways you would like to serve others in the future.

1) _____

_____

2) _____

_____

Explain why you have these desires.

1) _____

_____

2) _____

_____

List an immediate action you can take toward accomplishing your goals.

Goal 1 Action)_____

_____

Goal 2 Action)_____

_____

"Consciously or unconsciously, everyone renders some service. If we cultivate the habit of doing this service deliberately, our desire to serve others will steadily grow stronger, and we will achieve, not only happiness for ourselves, but also happiness for the world at large." ~ Mahatma Gandhi

Think your morning JUICE. Now maybe it's just me, but this sounds like a really good idea. Do you agree or disagree? For today's journal entry, read the quote, answer my question, and explain why you feel the way you do. Then describe your inspired thoughts and feelings.

Date: ____/____/____

Read the quote and answer my question. I disagree____ or I agree____! Explain why you feel the way you do.

_____

_____

_____

_____

Describe your inspired thoughts and feelings.

_____

_____

"We shall never know all the good a simple smile can do." ~ Mother Teresa

Think your morning JUICE. A simple smile is one of the easiest forms of help you can give. For today's journal entry, describe a few experiences when a simple smile from someone helped put a smile on your face. Then, look at the smiling and silly looking animal photographs and describe your inspired thoughts and feelings.

Date: ____/____/____

Describe a few experiences when a smile from someone helped put a smile on your face.

1) _____

_____

2) _____

_____

3) _____

_____

4) _____

_____

Look at the smiling and silly looking animal photographs and describe your inspired thoughts and feelings.

Picture 1)_____

_____

Picture 2)_____

_____

Picture 3)_____

_____

Picture 4)_____

_____

Exercise 9 - Mindset to Easily ask for Help: Three Premises and Three Results

Think your morning JUICE. Use this page to continue or redo Exercise 9. Then, when you have completed the exercise, describe your inspired thoughts and feelings

Date: _____ / _____ / _____

_____

_____

_____

_____

_____

_____

_____

_____

_____

_____

_____

_____

_____

_____

_____

_____

_____

_____

Post View

Andrewism: The Watch-Er - The Do-Er - The Be-Er Of Both

Some Watch The World & …

    Their Life Is An Out Of Body Non-Experience.

    They See The Stage, & Are An Audience For Everything. They Only Observe Others, & They Overlook Themselves.

Some Do The World & …

    Their Life Is All Acting, With All Around Action.

    They Manifest Their Motions, & Are An Activist For Everything.

    They Extremely Engage Experience, & Under Involve Their Inner-Selves.

Some Few, Balance Both. They're A Tandem Of The Two, & …

    Their Life Is An Encapsulated, Completely Embodied Experience.

    They Be The Theater, Audience, & Actor All Together.

    They're Awake & Alive. They See & Experience Life Holistically!

So,   With This Conditional Capacity Of A Human Seeing & Do-ing Both,

    Comes The Potential Possibility For Life Lessons To Be Learned & Used,

    In The Long-Term, Long Run, Of A Long-Lived-Life!

Think your morning JUICE. This *Andrewism* poetry piece, perfectly summarizes this chapter. It talks about Watch-Ers, people who are only being aware of their inactive life; Do-Ers, people who are only doing alive in their over-active life; and Be-Ers Of Both, people who are amazingly able to live mind-fully and mind-freely, both in the same life. For today's journal entry, read the *Andrewism* poetry piece, and describe your inspired thoughts and feelings. And, if you want, write your own, chapter-inspired, poetry piece. And if not, review a few, favorite chapter concepts, and continue to describe your inspired thoughts and feelings. When all that's done, continue our journey in Chapter 3: See the Scene!

Date: ____ / ____ / ____

Read the *Andrewism* poetry piece, and describe your inspired thoughts and feelings.

_____

_____

_____

_____

If you want, write your own, chapter-inspired, poetry piece.

Title:_____

_____

_____

_____

_____

_____

_____

_____

_____

_____

_____

Or review a few, favorite chapter concepts, and continue to describe your inspired thoughts and feelings.

1) _____

_____

2) _____

_____

3) _____

_____

4) _____

_____

Extra Expressings and Thoughtful Thinkings: Positivity Paragraphs

SOW SEEDS! BE THE FARMER OF FOREVER!
SEEDS: Not ONLY Your Children! They Are …
ALSO Your Thoughts! Feelings! & ALL Ideas!
& Ultimately ALL ALIVINGS! & ACTIONINGS!
ALL Your Kindnesses! & Compassions! AND
ALL Your Together-ings! & Teachings! AND
ALL Your Know-ings! & Show-ings! AND
ALL Your Encourage-ings! & Empower-ings!
Make ALL Your Positivity(s) Productivities!

Write your inspired thoughts and feelings.

_____
_____
_____
_____
_____
_____
_____
_____

TELL & SHOW: We all played the other way
round. But I believe this way is much more
sound. For so many, totally tell a great story!
But then, fail to show in their foretold future!
So I say, "If you truthfully tell a tale, and you
set a sail, for some pre-determined destination,
make sure you show a deal of determination!
Make sure actions show your story is TRUE!
& THIS WAY, LIFE DIS-PLAYS WHO IS YOU!"

Write your inspired thoughts and feelings.

_____
_____
_____
_____
_____
_____
_____
_____

EVERY DAY you wake up is a GOOD DAY!
EVERY DAY you can SORT your life full-ly!
Self: Fill YOUR heart with Love & Light!
Occupation: Do YOU with Purpose-Fullness!
Relationships: Keep them all Real &Alive!
Time-Transitions: It is not about quantity!
It is all about quality! Make it all moving!
Physically, Intellectually, Emotionally…
[& Especially] Spiritually! [ALL FOR YOU!]

Write your inspired thoughts and feelings.

_____
_____
_____
_____
_____
_____
_____
_____

Someone says, "So what's new with you?"
A+:)'s A: "Today! And time spent with you!"
Everyday is new! A present gift! Just for you!
This is true! As it is for you! It is for me!
Do you see? Truly, this is a great opportunity!
Today, think for yourself! Say, "I do see me!"
Today is a great-full day! Cause I get to be me!
And you get to be you! So give this to someone
you see worthy, of being fantastically friendly!

Write your inspired thoughts and feelings.

_____
_____
_____
_____
_____
_____
_____
_____

You Doing You: Your #1 Life-Long Job-Career!
Always Be Yourself! For all others are taken!
Always Remember: Doing Your Life is The Only
Occupation for which YOU are Overly Qualified!
It's literately The Part You Were Born To Play!
So play it with The ABCs of AN ALIVING LIFE!
An Attitude of GrAtitude for All Abundance!
A Boundless Bravery Beyond Bold-Full-Ness!
A Completely Compassionate Character: YOU!

Write your inspired thoughts and feelings.
_____
_____
_____
_____
_____
_____
_____
_____
_____

TOUGH TIMES & EMOTIONAL EXPERIENCES:
I see my sentiment, "Sorry for your now self."
I see your situation, stronger your now self is.
Present: More Emotional Depth You Will See!
Future: More Appreciative You Will Truly Be!
Humanitarianly: You Need Never Be Lone-ly!
As Long As I AM ME [A+!] UR Never Alone!
May You KNOW: My Heart Gives Great Hugs!
FROM EVERYWHERE: I AM BEHOLDING YOU!

Write your inspired thoughts and feelings.
_____
_____
_____
_____
_____
_____
_____
_____

MUSIC: Special Songs Spark Sentimental(s)!
Play-Lists Manifest Mind-Full Memories! It's …
Love Lost &/OR Firstly Finally Found! It's …
All About Making Life's Momentary Musicals!
AND ALSO Solidifying My Mind's Memorials!
This is the Soul's Soundtrack Safe Storage!
Life has rhythm, melodies, and harmonies!
When one finds radio stations & singers,
who match all life's moods, … It's Magical!

Write your inspired thoughts and feelings.
_____
_____
_____
_____
_____
_____
_____
_____

The HEART of YOUR BEHELD: This is by far
The BEST of ALL POSSIBLE WORLDS! For …
When one embraces as an act of ALIVING &
LOVING, Held-Beyond-Both's-Heartbeats, &
Done-With-Whole-Body-&-Soul, I defy anyone,
to identify and/or imagine, anyplace else,
they'd rather be, and/or even ever experience!
What I Wish 4U: May you fully find, A-LOVE-
A-LOT-FRIEND WHO DOES THIS FULLY-4-YOU!

Write your inspired thoughts and feelings.
_____
_____
_____
_____
_____
_____
_____
_____

117

Okay. Now turn the page.

CHAPTER 3:
SEE THE SCENE!

Preview

"The real voyage of discovery consists not in seeking new landscapes, but in having new eyes." ~ Marcel Proust

Think your morning JUICE. Welcome to Chapter 3: See the Scene! In 1928, Alexander Fleming, observed how a mold (penicillin) killed bad bacteria. This accidental discovery led to the incredible introduction of antibiotics. Since then, countless lives have been saved! (In 1949, this would include the then seven-year-old, far future, mother of me!) Now obviously way before Fleming arrived, everyone knew what mold looked like. But on this particular occasion Fleming saw it with specialized sight and with new eyes. He saw, and he made a new, unique connection which no one had ever made before. In short, Fleming traveled the "real voyage of discovery." For today's journal entry, do the following five writing prompts. (1) List a few favorite, famous, and historic world-changing discoveries and/or inventions. (2) Add two of your own presently un-famous ideas. (3) Describe how the items you listed in (1) influence your life. (4 & 5) Read the quote, review the book's chapter preview, and describe your inspired thoughts and feelings.

Date: _____/_____/_____

Do the Five writing prompts:

1) A)_____

   B)_____

   C)_____

   D)_____

2) E)_____

   F)_____

3) A)_____

   _____

   B)_____

   _____

C)_____

_____

D)_____

_____

4) & 5)_____

_____

_____

_____

_____

_____

_____

_____

_____

"Keep yourself clean and bright; you are the window through which you see the world."
~ George Bernard Shaw

Think your morning JUICE. This quote illustrates this chapter's paradigm. With all your specialized sights, the real "window through which you see" is your mind's eye. For today's journal entry, pick a number from 1-10, which represents how clean and bright you keep your world viewing windows. (1 is looking through a layer of dark dirt and 10 is looking through commercial clear, wonderfully washed windows.) Explain your answer and describe a few ideas for how you will potentially improve your specialized sights' score.

Date: ____/____/____

Pick a number from 1-10, which represents how clean and bright you keep your world viewing windows. _____ Explain your answer and describe a few ideas for how you will potentially improve your specialized sights' score.

_____

_____

_____

_____

1) _____

2) _____

3) _____

4) _____

Hindsight

"Write the wrongs done to you in sand. Write the goods on marble. Let go resentments and thoughts of retaliation and revenge. These diminish you. Hold on to gratitude and joy. These increase you." ~ Proverb

Think your morning JUICE. For today's journal entry, read the quote, along with the book's Hindsight section, and describe your inspired thoughts and feelings.

Date: ____/____/____

Read the quote, along with the book's Hindsight section, and describe your inspired thoughts and feelings.

_____

_____

_____

_____

_____

_____

"The world is won by those who let it go." ~ Lao Tzu

Think your morning JUICE. The idea behind this quote is, if you are able to forgive people and eventually let go of your psychological baggage, you will ultimately win the gift of an en-lite-ened present. For today's journal entry, list a few people who still psychologically weigh you down. Explain how they affect your daily life. Then ask yourself, "Do I want to strenuously continue spending an enormous amount of energy, venture way beyond my personal sphere of control, and actually attempt to fight, for a potentially unattainable, external justice? Or, do I want to easily control myself, and calm-cool-collected-and-confidently choose, to harmoniously have internal peace?" Well, when you put it that way!

So seriously, make the clear choice. Choose to forgive, and lovingly let go of the psychological baggage, which has been woefully weighing you down. Then, after you've gone through your positive, personal, and psychological en-lite-enment, describe your inspired thoughts and feelings.

Date: _____/_____/_____

List a few people who still psychologically weigh you down. (A) Explain how they affect your daily life. (B)

1A)_____ B) _____

_____

_____

_____

2A)_____ B) _____

_____

_____

_____

3A)_____ B) _____

_____

_____

_____

4A)_____ B) _____

_____

_____

_____

Then, after you've gone through your positive, personal, psychological en-lite-enment, describe your inspired thoughts and feelings.

_____

_____

_____

_____

Exercise 10 - Hind-Sight: A Special Task of Past Detoxification

Think your morning JUICE. Use this page to continue or redo Exercise 10. Then, when you have completed the exercise, describe your inspired thoughts and feelings.

Date: _____ / _____ / _____

_____

_____

_____

_____

_____

_____

_____

_____

_____

_____

_____

_____

_____

_____

_____

_____

_____

_____

_____

Foresight

"Creativity is like driving a car at night, you never see further than your headlights, but you can make the whole trip that way." ~ E. L. Doctorow

Think your morning JUICE. This is a brilliant quote, and I use it often with my creativity workshop students. When I decided to write this book and workbook, I knew this quote would fit perfectly in the Foresight section. For today's journal entry, read the quote and describe your inspired thoughts and feelings.

Date: ____/____/____

Read the quote and describe your inspired thoughts and feelings.

_____

_____

_____

_____

"Your imagination is your preview of life's coming attractions." ~ Albert Einstein

Think your morning JUICE. When you see the previews of a soon to be released movie you get a pretty good idea of what it's all about and what it's going to look like. The same goes for creative visualization. When you imagine your possible future with extreme detail, extensive description, and/or elaborately drawn depictions, it's a lot easier to believe what you imagine will be a positive, probable, future reality. For today's journal entry, describe a few, favorite creative visualization ideas. Be specific.

Date: ____/____/____

Describe a few, favorite creative visualization ideas. Be specific.

1) _____

_____

2) _____

_____

3) _____

_____

4) _____

_____

"Reality has limits. Imagination is boundless!" ~ Jean-Jacques Rousseau

Think your morning JUICE. I am always amazed at movie magic and special effects. I am especially impressed by sci-fi and fantasy movies. And I love it when someone's dramatic imagination eventually leads to real life inventions. For example, Alexander Graham Bell invented the telephone way back in 1876. And Gene Rodenberry, the creator of Star Trek, had the fantastic foresight to imagine a hand-held flip-top "communicator." Today we call these real-life gadgets cell/smart phones, I-pads, and portable computers. For today's journal entry, list a few favorite examples of when the past's techno-fantasy foresight became today's real-life reality. Explain why you appreciate these interesting and inspired inventions.

Date: ____/____/____

(A) List a few, favorite examples of when the past's, techno-fantasy fore-sight, became today's real-life reality. (B) Explain why you appreciate these interesting items and inspired invention ideas.

1A)_____ B) _____

_____

2A)_____ B) _____

_____

3A)_____ B) _____

_____

4A)_____ B) _____

_____

"In every block of marble I see a statue as plain as though it stood before me, shaped and perfect in attitude and action. I have only to hew away the rough walls that imprison the lovely apparition to reveal it to other eyes as mine see it." ~ Michelangelo

Think your morning JUICE. I like this quote for two reasons. First, I enjoy descriptions of artistic foresight. It is inspirational how artists visualize a desired result and then creatively manifest their visualization. Second, the quote reminds me of a funny, novelty item I once saw in a garden supply store. It was a brick shaped rock, with a smooth faced side. The rock was engraved with big, bold block letters… **NOTHING IS WRITTEN IN STONE!"**

For today's journal entry, write your thoughts and feelings on the concept of artistic foresight. And if you've ever seen any funny novelty items like the imprinted irony rock, then describe the items and write about where they were found. Lastly, look at the next photograph and describe your inspired thoughts and feelings.

Date: ____/____/____

Write your thoughts and feelings on the concept of artistic foresight.

_____

_____

_____

_____

_____

_____

Describe any funny novelty items you've seen and write about where they were found.

1) _____

_____

_____

_____

2) _____

_____

_____

_____

Look at the next photograph and describe your inspired thoughts and feelings.

_____

_____

_____

_____

_____

_____

Now-Sight

Andrewism: For The Love Of The Game

As If It Were On The Hip Seam Of A Sexy, Silk Night Gown,
The Buzzer Beater, B-Ball, Glides Gracefully, The God-Like, Game Clock, Clicks.
Up …

The Just Journey Is A, "J-Tre.'" The Ball's Rotation Is Reversed, Seemingly In Slow Motion.
The Hopeful, Home Crowd, Collectively Holds Its' Breath.

Arc's Climax …

If Hail Mary Is Truly Full Of Grace, Then The B-Ball's Divinely Desired Destination,
Would Be Famously Found, & The, "A+" Audience, Will Explode With Applauded Approval.

Down …

All That Is Required For A Hero's Valiant Victory, Is A Single Shot, Sensational Score:
A.K.A "A Championship Finals, Fantastic Finish!"

Swish!! …   "Thank You!" Michael Jordan

P.S. Thank You Karim Abdul Jabar, Larry Bird, Kobe Bryant, Wilt Chamberlain, Caitlin Clark, Stephen Curry, Julius Erving, Magic Johnson, Shaquille O'Neil, and Oscar Robinson; Lou Gehrig, Derek Jeter, Jackie Robinson, Cal Ripken Jr., Babe Ruth, Nolan Ryan, and Ichiro Suzuki; Muhammad Ali and James Braddock; Jim Brown, Bo Jackson, Vince Lombardy, Walter Payton, Jerry Rice, Deion Sanders, and Lawrence Taylor; Peggy Fleming and Scott Hamilton; Anika Sorensen and Tiger Woods; Wayne Gretzky and Steve Yzerman; Tony Hawk; Mia Hamm and Pele; Arthur Ashe, Billy Jean King, and Serena Williams; Kotch Kari; Greg Louganis; Michael Phelps; Simone Biles and Nadia Comaneci; Usain Bolt, Jackie Joyner Kersee, Carl Lewis, Edwin Moses, Jessie Owens, Wilma Rudolph, and Jim Thorp; Shawn White; Bonnie Blair and Eric Heiden; & MANY MORE!

Think your morning JUICE. For today's journal entry, read the Now-Sight book section, and the *Andrewism* poetry piece. Describe your inspired thoughts and feelings.

Date: ____/____/____

Read the Now-Sight book section, and the *Andrewism* poetry piece. Describe your inspired thoughts and feelings.

_____

_____

_____

_____

BEAUTIFUL Insight

Andrewism: -A Car-

-A Car With Light Speed-
-A Car With Cool Color-
-A Car With Concubine Curves-
-A Car With Hawk Headlights-
-A Car With Futuristic Features-
-A Car With Cockpit Console-
-A Car With Soul-
-A Car With Surprise-
-A Car With Suspense-
-A Car With Sexy-
-A Car With Sleek-
-A Car With Sophistication-
-A Car With Personalized Personality-
-A Car With Mechanical Heartlessness-
-A Car With …
-A Human Driver … This Makes All The Difference!

Think your morning JUICE. This *Andrewism* poetry piece is my response to every car commercial ever made, and it's my way of saying, "It's what's on the inside that counts. And that's what should make all the difference." For today's journal entry, read the *Andrewism* poetry piece, and read the book section. Then describe your inspired thoughts and feelings. (Note: This book section covers several concepts which I'll address in greater detail in upcoming entries. For now, simply write about your general thoughts and feelings.)

Date: ____/____/____

Read the *Andrewism* poetry piece, and the new book section. Describe your inspired thoughts and feelings.

_____

_____

_____

_____

_____

_____

"The most visible joy only reveals itself when we've transformed it, from within."
~ Rainer Maria Rilke

Think your morning JUICE. Do you agree or disagree? For today's journal entry, answer this question and explain your answer. Then, write about a few examples of evidence, which substantiate your position.

Date: ____/____/____

Do you agree or disagree? I _____. Explain your answer.

_____

_____

_____

_____

_____

_____

Write about a few examples of evidence, which substantiate your position.

1) _____

2) _____

3) _____

4) _____

"No one is laughable who is able to laugh at themselves." ~ Seneca

Think your morning JUICE. The ability to laugh at oneself is an invaluable character trait. It is the highest form of in-sight. For today's journal entry, describe a few examples when you in-sight-fully laughed at yourself.

Date: ____/____/____

Describe a few examples when you in-sight-fully laughed at yourself.

1) _____

_____

_____

_____

2) _____

_____

_____

_____

3) _____

_____

_____

_____

4) _____

_____

_____

_____

"It is hard to fight an enemy who has outposts in your head." ~ Sally Kempton

Think your morning JUICE. Anyone with an awfully loud and sadly self-defeating, inner-critic, will easily empathies with this quote. If you do, then for today's journal entry, write about a time when your inner-critic was diabolically debilitating. If you don't, write about how you were able to silence, or at least turn down the volume, on your inner-critic. And by the way, "Congratulations!" (If you want to write about both, feel free.)

Date: _____/_____/_____

Write about a time when your inner-critic was diabolically debilitating.

_____

_____

_____

_____

Write about how you were able to silence, or at least turn down the volume, on your inner-critic.

_____

_____

_____

_____

"Play is the exultation of the possible." ~ Martin Buber

Think your morning JUICE. For today's journal entry, review a few of your set goals. Then describe how your inner-child will play with the possible or, as previously stated, the probable.

Date: ____/____/____

Describe how your inner-child will play with the possible or, as previously stated, the probable. Write your goal (A) and plan your play. (B)

1A)_____

_____

1B)_____

_____

2A)_____

_____

2B)_____

_____

3A)_____

_____

3B)_____

_____

4A)_____

_____

4B)_____

_____

"The most potent muse of all, is our own inner-child." ~ Stephen Nachmanovitch

Think your morning JUICE. I love how this quote casts our inner-child, as our greatest teacher, or our "most potent muse." For today's journal entry, describe a few times when you let your inner-child loose (A), you amazingly allowed yourself to participate in a life changing experience (B), and you surprisingly had a whole lot of fun! (C)

Date: ____/____/____

Describe a few times when you did (A), (B), and (C).

1) _____

_____

_____

_____

2) _____

_____

_____

_____

3) _____

_____

_____

_____

4) _____

_____

_____

_____

"Every child is an artist. The problem is to remain one, once they grow up." ~ Pablo Picasso

Think your morning JUICE. Picasso was a very famous artist. So when he says listen to your inner-child and remain an artist once you grow up, I'd follow his advice. For today's journal entry, write about a few times when you were artistic. As you recall these events, describe your inspired thoughts and feelings. Remember, practically any creative exercise or activity can count as artistic.

Date: ____/____/____

Write about a few times when you were artistic. Describe your inspired thoughts and feelings.

1) _____

_____

_____

_____

2) _____

_____

_____

_____

3) _____

_____

_____

_____

4) _____

_____

_____

_____

"To be independent of public opinion, is the first, formal condition of achieving anything great." ~ G.W. F. Hegel

Think your morning JUICE. This quote reminds me to be passionately self-empowered, confident, and trust my inner-champion and highest self. For today's journal entry, answer the question, "Do you agree or disagree with the quote?" Explain your answer. If you want, describe an experience, which supports your position.

Date: ____/____/____

Do you agree or disagree with this quote? I _____. Explain your answer.

_____

_____

_____

_____

"Like an ability or muscle, hearing your inner wisdom is strengthened by repetition."
~ Robbie Gass

Think your morning JUICE. This quote encourages you to hear your Inner-Champion and your Inner-Highest Self. For today's journal entry, describe a few times when you heard, and trusted, your positive, inner voices. Explain how this mental ability became easier each time you did it.

Date: _____/_____/_____

Describe a few times when you heard, *and trusted*, your positive, inner-voices.

1) _____

_____

2) _____

_____

3) _____

_____

4) _____

_____

Explain how this mental "ability" became easier each time you did it.

_____

_____

_____

_____

_____

_____

"Remember, you are the only one who thinks inside your mind! You are the power, and the authority, in your world." ~ Louise Hay

Think your morning JUICE. This quote reminds me of a personal promise. With my inner-champion and inner-highest self I say, "These voices will always be my final answers. These voices will always get the last word." For today's journal entry, read the quote and consider the concept from the book section. Then do a truly self-affirming action. Make the same promise to yourself. Finally, describe your inspired thoughts and feelings.

Date: ____/____/____

_____
_____
_____
_____
_____
_____

Once we've developed a relationship with our inner teachers, we will always have access to an unwavering source of clarity, wisdom, and guidance!" ~ Shakti Gawain

Think your morning JUICE. This quote parallels the inner-integrity concept. Think of your inner-teachers as your gut feelings. And when you do periodic gut-checks, the benefits are, "clarity, wisdom, and guidance." For today's journal entry, describe a few times when you listened to your gut feelings. Explain how this helped your decision-making process and write about your results.

Date: ____/____/____

Describe a few times when you listened to your gut feelings.

1) _____
_____

2) _____
_____

3) _____
_____

4) _____
_____

Explain how listening to your gut feelings helped your decision-making process and write about your results.

_____

_____

_____

_____

"I call intuition cosmic fishing. You feel the nibble, but you have to hook and catch the fish yourself." ~ Buckminster Fuller

Think your morning JUICE. So go fish! Revisit a few favorite intuitive ideas and figuratively continue to "hook and catch the fish yourself." For today's journal entry, read the quote, consider the intuitive process of idea creation, and describe your inspired thoughts and feelings.

Date: _____/_____/_____

Read the quote, consider the intuitive process of idea creation, and describe your inspired thoughts and feelings.

_____

_____

_____

_____

Holistic Intimacy and The Hierarchy of Human Sexuality

"Love is the discovery of ourselves in others, and the delight in the recognition."
~ Alexander Smith

Think your morning JUICE. This quote perfectly parallels the concept of Intimacy (In-To-Me-You-See). And if you've ever been truly in love, I'm sure you relate to this idea. For today's journal entry, write about a time, or times, when you were, or are, in love with someone. Describe how you recognize yourself, in the other person.

Date: ____/____/____

Write about a time, or times, when you were, or are, in love with someone. Describe how you recognize yourself in the other person. (Put in your own numbers to separate one time from another.)

_____

_____

_____

_____

_____

_____

_____

_____

_____

_____

_____

_____

_____

_____

_____

_____

_____

"Physically pretty people are plenty.
Socially special people are surrounding us.
Intellectually indubitable people are infinite.
Mentally mammoth people are many.
But real-ly BEAUTIFUL people are really rare!
They are Love-A-Lots!
They love a lot and they should be loved a lot!" ~ Andrew S. Taylor

Think your morning JUICE. Remember this section from the book. The word BEAUTIFUL real-ly means (The ability to) Be (yourself), Enlightened, Alive, Unique, Trustworthy, Intelligent, Faith-Full, and Unconditionally Loving! Do you agree or disagree with the quote and the book section's concept? For today's journal entry, explain your answer.

Date: ____/____/____

Do you agree or disagree? Explain your answer. I _____.

_____

_____

_____

_____

"Poor is the woman whose pleasures depends on the permission of another." ~ Madonna

Think your morning JUICE. Madonna has re-invented her public and private self, countless times. So when I read this quote I immediately saw it as expert advice. I believe Madonna is saying, you need to rely primarily on yourself as the origin source for a positive self-image and a positive sense of self-esteem. Do you agree or disagree? For today's journal entry, write and explain your answer. Then, trust your inner-champion and your inner-highest self, and describe your old, or new, positive self-image and positive sense of self-esteem.

Date: ____/____/____

Do you agree or disagree with Madonna's advice? Write and explain your answer.

_____

_____

_____

_____

Describe your old, or new, positive self-image and positive sense of self-esteem.

_____

_____

_____

_____

Learn Life Lessons: School Is Always In Session!

"The Rules For Being Human …
You will receive a body.
You will learn life lessons.
There are no mistakes.
A lesson is repeated until it is learned.
Learning life lessons never ends.
There is no better than here.
Others are merely mirrors of you.
What you make of your life is entirely up to you.
All answers can be found within the self.
To be a human being you must by nature be humane." ~ Cherie Carter-Scott

Think your morning JUICE. For today's journal entry, read The Rules For Being Human … quote and do the writing prompts. First, describe your initial impression of each rule. Second, describe your overall reaction to the list. And third, write any additional rules you feel are missing. When you're done, describe your inspired thoughts and feelings.

Date: _____/_____/_____

Describe your initial impression of each rule.

1) _____

_____

_____

_____

2) _____

_____

_____

_____

3) _____

_____

_____

_____

4)

5)

6)

7)

8)

9)

10)

Describe your overall reaction to the list.

_____

_____

_____

_____

Write any additional rules you feel are missing.

11) _____

_____

12) _____

_____

When you're done, describe your inspired thoughts and feelings.

_____

_____

_____

_____

_____

_____

"Pain is inevitable. Suffering is optional." ~ M. Kathleen Casey

Think your morning JUICE. This quote is the origin of Life Lesson 2. I've heard and said this quote countless times. For today's journal entry, read Life Lesson 1 and 2 and describe your inspired thoughts and feelings.

Date: ____/____/____

Read Life Lesson 1 and Life Lesson 2. Describe your inspired thoughts and feelings.

Life lesson 1) _____

_____

_____

_____

_____

_____

Life lesson 2)_____

_____

_____

_____

_____

_____

"I merely took the energy it takes to pout and I wrote some blues." ~ Duke Ellington

Think your morning JUICE. This quote perfectly parallels the previous, "Pain is inevitable. Suffering is optional," Casey quote. For today's journal entry, continue to contemplate the quotes' life lessons and continue to describe your inspired thoughts and feelings.

Date: _____/_____/_____

Continue to contemplate the quotes' life lessons and continue to describe your inspired thoughts and feelings.

_____

_____

_____

_____

"What does not kill me makes me stronger." ~ Albert Camus

Think your morning JUICE. This quote is the origin of Life Lesson 3. For today's journal entry, read the quote and book section and (1) describe your inspired thoughts and feelings. Then, write about a very painful memory. (2) And since you've survived, and moved forward beyond it, explain how it's made you a stronger person. (3)

Date: _____/_____/_____

1) _____

_____

_____

_____

2) _____

_____

_____

_____

3) _____

_____

_____

_____

"A woman is like a like a tea bag; you never know how strong it is until it's in hot water."
~ Eleanor Roosevelt

Think your morning JUICE. For today's journal entry, describe a few more examples, which parallel the previous three quotes. Explain why each example fits.

Date: _____/_____/_____

Write about a few more examples, which parallel the previous three quotes. Explain why each example fits.

1) _____

_____

_____

_____

_____

_____

2) _____

_____

_____

_____

_____

_____

3) _____

_____

_____

_____

_____

_____

4) _____

_____

_____

_____

_____

_____

"In the middle of difficulty lies opportunity." ~ Albert Einstein

Think your morning JUICE. Now we all know Albert Einstein was a fairly intelligent representative of the human race. So the next time you find yourself in a difficult situation, change your point of view and keep this quote in mind. Instead of seeing your situation as a problem, obstacle, or difficulty see it as an opportunity. Truly believe you will take advantage of it successfully. For today's journal entry, describe a couple examples when you made this mental transposition and explain how achieving a successful result changed your life.

Date: _____/_____/_____

Describe your examples and explain your life changing results.

1) _____

_____

_____

_____

2) _____

_____

_____

_____

"Do not fear mistakes - there are none." ~ Miles Davis

Think your morning JUICE. This quote parallels the third Rules For Being Human. It's also used in the book. So remember, "There are no mistakes, only learning opportunities." For today's journal entry, read the quote, consider the concept, and describe your inspired thoughts and feelings. Also, describe a couple moments when you applied the concept in your daily life.

Date: ____/____/____

Read the quote, consider the concept, and describe your inspired thoughts and feelings.

_____

_____

_____

_____

Describe a couple moments when you applied the concept in your daily life.

1) _____

_____

_____

_____

2) _____

_____

_____

_____

"If I could wish for my life to be perfect, it would be tempting, but I'd have to decline, for life would no longer teach me anything." ~ Allyson Jones

Think your morning JUICE. I included this quote for two reasons. First, it reminds you how your life is already perfect. You are A Perfect You. And you are this Perfect You because you've survived, and ultimately taken advantage of, a lifetime of learning opportunities. Second, it reinforces the concept of how life is a teacher and school is always in session. For today's journal entry, read the quote, consider the concept, and continue to describe your inspired thoughts and feelings.

Date: _____/_____/_____

Read the quote, consider the concept, and continue to describe your inspired thoughts and feelings.

_____

_____

_____

_____

_____

_____

"Learn to wish everything in life should come to pass exactly as it does." ~ Epictetus

Think your morning JUICE. The previous quote described a wish, which should be declined. This quote presents a wish, which should be embraced. It is incredibly ironic, because unlike most wishes, it is guaranteed to come true. For today's journal entry, read the quote and describe your inspired thoughts and feelings.

Date: _____/_____/_____

Read the quote and describe your inspired thoughts and feelings.

_____

_____

_____

_____

_____

_____

"Creative activity is a process of learning, where teacher and pupil are located in the same individual." ~ Arthur Koestler

Think your morning JUICE. I am always amazed when I see a student suddenly understand and internalize a concept. Then, they're able to quickly turn around, and externally apply the concept in their daily life. A prime example is the use of conflict resolution words. Elementary age children are taught a script of words to use when they have a problem with peers. At first, the words are out of context, but then the child uses the words properly in a classroom or the playground. For today's journal entry, explain how you learned a couple important life lessons, and describe how you turned around and appropriately applied the lessons in your daily life.

Date: _____/_____/_____

Explain how you learned a couple important life lessons.

Life lesson 1)_____

_____

_____

_____

Life lesson 2)_____

_____

_____

_____

Describe how you turned around and appropriately applied the lessons in your daily life.

Life lesson 1)_____

_____

_____

_____

Life lesson 2)_____

_____

_____

_____

"It's a funny thing about life; if you refuse to accept anything but the best, most often you will get it." ~ Somerset Maugham

Think your morning JUICE. What's this quote's life lesson? For today's journal entry, read the quote, answer the writing prompt question, and describe your inspired thoughts and feelings.

Date: _____/_____/_____

Read the quote, answer the writing prompt question, and describe your inspired thoughts and feelings.

_____

_____

_____

_____

"This is a story about four people named Everybody, Somebody, Anybody, and Nobody. There was an important job that needed to be done, and Everybody was sure that Somebody would do it. Anybody could have done it but Nobody ended up doing it. Somebody got angry about that, because it was Everybody's job. Everybody thought Anybody could do it but Nobody realized that Everybody wouldn't do it. It ended up that Everybody blamed Somebody when Nobody did what Anybody could have done in the first place." ~ Author Unknown

Think your morning JUICE. What's this quote's life lesson? For today's journal entry, read the quote, answer the writing prompt question, and describe your inspired thoughts and feelings.

Date: ____/____/____

Read the quote, answer the writing prompt question, and describe your inspired thoughts and feelings.

_____

_____

_____

_____

_____

_____

Post View

"There is no end to the adventures we can have, if we seek them with both eyes open."
~ Nehru

Think your morning JUICE. This quote reminds me to, "seek adventures with both eyes open" and it inspires me to keep an open mind whenever I use my specialized sights. For today's journal entry, read the quote and describe your inspired thoughts and feelings.

Date: ____/____/____

Read the quote and describe your inspired thoughts and feelings.

_____

_____

_____

_____

_____

_____

"What lies behind us and what lies before us, are tiny matters when compared to what lies within us." ~ Ralph Waldo Emerson

Think your morning JUICE. For today's journal entry, answer each question.

Date: ____/____/____

When you look back with Hindsight what do you see?

_____

_____

_____

_____

When you look forward with Foresight what do you see?

_____

_____

_____

_____

When you look inside with Insight what do you see?

_____

_____

_____

_____

When others see with Intimacy (In-To-Me-You-See) what do they see? (If you don't know it's time to ask.)

_____

_____

_____

_____

"There is no need to run outside for better seeing, … Rather abide at the center of your being; … Search your heart and see." ~ Lao Tzu

Think your morning JUICE. This quote parallels the movie and song concepts discussed in the book: seeing clearly with better eyes. For today's journal entry, read the quote, consider the concepts, view the next photograph, and describe your inspired thoughts and feelings.

Date: ____/____/____

Read the quote, consider the concepts, view the photograph, and describe your inspired thoughts and feelings.

_____

_____

_____

_____

"The student has hindsight; the teacher has foresight; the master has insight. In the school of daily life, you are here to become a student, a teacher, and a master. You are here to become someone who learns from the past, foresees the consequences of your actions, and finally, looks within, to discover how the Universe is always presenting itself in the present." ~ Dan Millman

Think your morning JUICE. This quote perfectly parallels several concepts from the chapter. For today's journal entry, continue to consider the chapter concepts and describe your inspired thoughts and feelings. For future reference create a title for each concept.

Date: _____ / _____ / _____

Continue to consider chapter concepts and describe your inspired thoughts and feelings.

Concept title 1)_____

_____

_____

_____

_____

_____

Concept title 2)_____

_____

_____

_____

_____

_____

"Our demons are our limitations, which shut us off from the realization the of the ubiquity of the spirit… each of these demons is conquered in a vision quest." ~ Joseph Campbell

"Vision Quests are an age-old human practice for grooming your spirit."
~ Brooke Medicine Eagle

Think your morning JUICE. I was introduced to the concept of a vision quest by a movie of the same name. It inspired me to find out more. Participating in a literal or metaphorical quest or inner journey is a common theme in movies because they mirror what happens naturally in life. What event has prompted you to grow? Describe the event and the growth you experienced.

Choose a few favorite concepts from the chapter, review the sections, and since you've already had time to process the concepts, describe your newly inspired thoughts and feelings. Then continue our journey in Chapter 4: Set The Stage!

Date: ____/____/____

1) _____

_____

_____

_____

2) _____
_____
_____
_____

3) _____
_____
_____
_____

4) _____
_____
_____
_____

Andrew's Afterthoughts: Writing this self-help book and workbook has been my greatest and most intense inner journey. The experience has extremely exceeded all my expectations and has gone way beyond being bountifully beneficial. In short, it's been a wholly joyful journey and an amazing, life-long, dramatic dream come true. Use these lines to brainstorm, outline, and plan your own future joyful journeys.

_____
_____
_____
_____
_____
_____
_____
_____
_____
_____
_____

Extra Expressings and Thoughtful Thinkings: Positivity Paragraphs

DREAMS: THESE ARE DESTINIES TO DO!
In our mind's eye, we imagine what we are
inspired to envision. WE ARE CREATIVES!
In our heart's eye, we search & feel our way!
With persistence & passion, we positively
produce empowered productions of our lives!
So when you dream, see it all for what it is!
Your divinely determined destination! … BUT
REMEMBER, MAKE THE JOURNEY JOY-FULL!

Write your inspired thoughts and feelings.

_____
_____
_____
_____
_____
_____
_____
_____

TODAY: LIVE ON PURPOSE! DO YOU BEAUTIFUL!
Be Yourself! ONLY YOU can play you perfectly!
Enlightened! Healthy Heart & Mind: Light-Full!
Alive! Don't make a living! Live an ALIVING!
Unique! Defiantly do your un-common character!
Trustworthy! Keep Promises! Always Accountable!
Intelligent! Book, Street, & In All Social Situations!
Faithful! In BOTH Spiritual & Your Soul-Full Self!
Unconditionally **L**oving! A True-For-You-Heart-Set!

Write your inspired thoughts and feelings.

_____
_____
_____
_____
_____
_____
_____
_____

ME-MESSANGER! Here's what I have to say!
OU ARE:) A LIGHT-EST OF THE UNIVERSE!
YOU ARE:) A BRIGHTEST OF ALL BULBS!
YOU ARE:) A STRONGEST OF ALL SOULS!
YOU ARE:) A BEST OF ALL BEHELDS!
YOU ARE:) A MOST OF ALL BEAUTI-FULLS!
YOU ARE:) A MANIFEST OF ALL MAGICALS!
YOU ARE:) A MIRACLE OF ALL NATURALS!
YOU ARE:) A LOVE-ABLE-A-LOT-EST OF ALLS!

Write your inspired thoughts and feelings.

_____
_____
_____
_____
_____
_____
_____
_____

LOVE: WE ALL KNOW IT WHEN WE FEEL IT!
& When we feel it, we should easily express it!
For it's ALWAYS ALL RIGHT! When it's TRUE!
Looks are on a level. BEAUTIFUL IS DEEPER!
It's seeing-hearing with your heart's eyes-ears!
It's extremely empowering emotion, GREATER
than the sum of all its individual ingredients!
So I say for you to do: As it is for You, Friends,
& Family, AS ONLY YOU CAN DO, LOVE TRUE!

Write your inspired thoughts and feelings.

_____
_____
_____
_____
_____
_____
_____
_____

4We: What I want 4Me & 4Thee, is 4Us 2Be!
4Today: May we LOVE, the rightest of ways!
4We: May we LIVE, instants of immortalities!
4Now: May we 4EVER KNOW, heroically how!
4We: May we SOUL-FULL-LY SEE, simplicity!
4Surely, safety, security, & sweet serenity!
4We: May we always be, abundance aplenty!
4Mes: May we graciously give, fortunes freely!
4We: May we Live, Happily, Ever After, Truly!

Present Pleasantries! [NOT Fortune Cookies!]
Why wait for futures to message mouth-fulls?
Sweet Sentiments! Say them all TODAY! NOW!
Some savor thoughts & feelings but don't say.
I say, SHOUT ALL ALIVE LOVINGS OUT LOUD!
If my message is A CUTENESS or A KINDNESS,
I say, CONVEY IT ALL WITH NO-TIME-MISSED!
Make sure all your mind's magical morsels are
heard from your heart, and made into meals!

Write your inspired thoughts and feelings.
_____
_____
_____
_____
_____
_____
_____
_____

Write your inspired thoughts and feelings.
_____
_____
_____
_____
_____
_____
_____

Okay. Now turn the page.

CHAPTER 4:
SET THE STAGE!

Preview

"Out of clutter; find simplicity." ~ Albert Einstein

Think your morning JUICE. I begin Chapter 4: Set The Stage! with this quote because both are about how to organize your life. In the first section, SORT Your Life Into a Four-File System, I talk about claiming Self, solo-time, learning Occupation, time management tips, living The ABCs Of Successful Relationships, and establishing a foundation of Time-Transitions. For today's journal entry, read the chapter's Preview and describe your inspired thoughts and feelings.

Date: _____/_____/_____

Read the quote, and the chapter's Preview, and describe your inspired thoughts and feelings.

_____

_____

_____

_____

_____

_____

SORT Your Life Into A Four-File System

"The greatest gift you can give yourself, is a little bit of your own attention!"
~ Anthony J. D'Angelo

Think your morning JUICE. In Chapter 1 you read about what it means to focus and pay attention. Now it's time to apply this knowledge in your daily life. As soon as possible, give yourself a greatest gift. Take yourself on a Solo-Time Artist Date. (See The Recommended Reading List on my website to find *The Artist Way* by Julia Cameron.) For today's journal entry, describe what you did on your date (A) and describe your inspired thoughts and feelings (B).

Date: _____/_____/_____

A)_____

_____

B)_____

_____

Andrewism: The Stationary Traveler

I Am Still.
It Is Anytime.
I Am In-Mind.
It Is Imagination Time.
I Am Anywhere.
It Is Free Fare.
I Am A Frequent Flyer.
It Is Easy Escapism.
I Am Anyone.
It Is A Medley Of Me-Isms.
I Am A Positive Life Force.
It Is A Dare To Be Great Situation.
I Am Being An Alive Human Doing!   I Am!
It Is A Trip Through The TaylorED Time, Life FANTASTIC!   It Is!

Think your morning JUICE. This *Andrewism* poetry piece, is about Self, solo-time. It is my way of expressing how your mind wanders and you easily become a stationary traveler. For today's journal entry, read the poetry piece and describe your inspired thoughts and feelings. Then use the next photograph as majestic motivation for a magical meditation. And when you're done, write about your new, solo-time experience.

Date: ____/____/____

Read the poetry piece, and describe your inspired thoughts and feelings.

_____

_____

_____

_____

_____

_____

Write about your new, solo-time experience.

_____

_____

_____

_____

"The greatest gift you can give yourself, is a little bit of your own attention!"
~ Anthony J. D'Angelo

Think your morning JUICE. In Chapter 1 you read about what it means to focus and pay attention. Now it's time to apply this knowledge in your daily life. As soon as possible, give yourself a greatest gift. Take yourself on a Solo-Time Artist Date. (See The Recommended Reading List on my website to find *The Artist Way* by Julia Cameron.) For today's journal entry, describe what you did on your date (A) and describe your inspired thoughts and feelings (B).

Date: _____ / _____ / _____

_____

_____

_____

_____

"It is only in the intentional silence of vigil and meditation, or in the quiet places of nature, that we encounter the song of the universe. Like the wind through the trees, this song echoes along the pathways of the cosmic web. It includes the celestial spinning of the planets, as well as the hum of all animals and the dancing song of all the plants. It includes the songs and spirits of all of the ancestors, as well as the beatings of all our collective hearts." ~ Caitlin Matthews

"To the mind that is still, the whole universe surrenders." ~ Lao Tzu

Think your morning JUICE. I once heard someone say, "Every point in the universe can be considered its center." My thought was, _That means when someone acts as if they are the center of the universe, they are in some small way right! And the only real problem with their presumed belief is that everyone else is also the center of the universe at the exact same time._ For today's journal entry, give yourself permission to be egocentric. Sit silently and indulge in a short, mind-free meditation. Then read the two quotes, consider the center of the universe concept, recall your new solo-time experience, and describe your inspired thoughts and feelings.

Date: ____/____/____

Read the two quotes and consider the center of the universe concept and …

_____

_____

… recall your new solo-time experience and …

_____

_____

… describe your inspired thoughts and feelings.

_____

_____

_____

_____

"Through vibration, harmony, tone, melody and meaning, music stimulates within us a direct experience of expanded reality." ~ Barbara Marx Hubbard

"Take a music bath. It is to the soul what a water-bath is to the body."
~ Oliver Wendell Holmes

Andrewism: The Ear & The Eye
The Past & The Present
The Magic & The Moment

My Musical Ear Tunes The Radio.
The Speakers Create Sound Surrounded.
My Mind's Eye Visualizes The Associations.
The Soul Transposes Emotions Energized.
My Past Experiences Encompass The, "Today-Self."
The Body Manifests Behavior Bio-Illogical.
My Present Continually Gives Birth, To Each "New-Now."
The Magical Moment Is Reality Sur-Realized.
My Time Travels, And My Journey Is Joyous.
The Title Is Traversed.

Andrewism: Music Matters!

The Variety Of Music Is Beyond Imagination.
The Variety Of Settings Is Equal As It Is Endless.
The Variety Of Audience Is Altogether Amazingly Astronomical.
        Okay, Obviously Music Maters.
What Should We Do Now?
What Should We Do Now That We've Heard This Musical Message?
Why You Should Go Forth And Listen Of Course!

Think your morning JUICE. These two quotes and *Andrewism* poetry pieces all share a common theme: Music. For today's journal entry, read the quotes and poetry pieces and describe your inspired thoughts and feelings. For the first quote, address the question, "How does music affect your life?" For the second quote, describe your idea of a, "music bath." Then, after following the writing prompts for the poetry pieces, if you're so inclined, write your own musically inspired, poetry piece. Finally, look at the next photograph and describe the type of music, and/or list the specific songs, which come to mind. Explain your answers.

Date: _____/_____/_____

Read the quotes and poetry pieces and describe your inspired thoughts and feelings.

Quote 1: How does music affect your life?) _____

_____

_____

Quote 2: What is your idea of a, "music bath?") _____

_____

_____

Andrewism 1) _____

_____

_____

Andrewism 2) _____

_____

_____

If you feel so inclined, write your own musically inspired poetry piece.

Title:_____

_____

_____

_____

_____

_____

_____

_____

_____

_____

_____

_____

Look at the next photograph. Describe the type of music, and/or list the specific songs, which come to mind.

_____

_____

_____

_____

Explain your answers.

_____

_____

_____

_____

"When I am, as it were, completely myself, entirely alone, and of good cheer … then ideas flow best, and most abundantly. Whence and how they come, I know not, nor can I force them." ~ Mozart

Think your morning JUICE. Mozart was notorious for writing music as if he was taking straight dictation. His ideas flowed and he'd write the music exactly as he heard it in his head. I think it is interesting how he says he needed to be, "completely (himself,) entirely alone, and of good cheer, (for the) ideas (to) flow best." For today's journal entry, follow Mozart's lead and see what happens. Set aside some solo-time when you can do something, which is special and unique for you. In short, do an activity where you feel completely yourself. Then put a smile on your face, be of good cheer, and describe a couple ideas, which are inspired in this special session of solo-time.

Date: _____/_____/_____

Describe a couple ideas, which are inspired in this special session of solo-time.

1) _____

_____

_____

_____

2) _____

_____

_____

_____

Exercise 11 - Daily-Debriefing: A Present Detoxification Process

Think your morning JUICE. Use this page to continue or redo Exercise 11. Then, when you have completed the exercise, describe your inspired thoughts and feelings.

Date: _____/_____/_____

_____

_____

_____

_____

_____

_____

_____

_____

_____

_____

_____

"Saying 'No!' can be the ultimate act of self-care." ~ Claudia Black

Think your morning JUICE. This quote is a perfect segue between the chapter's Self and Occupations sections. Because, if you look around, I am sure you will see quite a few occupational, mega-multitaskers. And you, might be guilty of indulging in this common condition. You need to know mega-multitasking can be very stressful. Over time, stress is one of the leading contributing factors in developing many major health problems. So saying "NO!" to doing just one more tiny task, might be the difference between satisfactorily completing your "DO TODAY!" list, or you suffering from one, or from any number of, stress induced ailments. For today's journal entry, describe a time when you said "No." Explain why you believe it was a healthy and productive act of self-care.

Date: ____/____/____

Describe a time when you said "No." Explain why you believe it was a healthy and productive act of self-care.

_____

_____

_____

_____

_____

_____

_____

_____

_____

_____

_____

"Despite several decades of research, the most effective way to predict vocational choice is simply to ask (a) person what (they) want (to do.)" ~ John Holland

Think your morning JUICE. Okay. Here goes, "If you could do absolutely any job or career, which one would you want to do?" For today's journal entry, write about two real job or careers you'd like to do and explain why. Then describe your ideal, dream job or career. Compare and contrast all three occupations.

Date: ____/____/____

Write about two real jobs or careers you'd like to do (A) and explain why. (B)

1A)_____ 1B) _____

_____

2A)_____ 2B) _____

_____

Describe your ideal, dream job or career. (A)

_____

_____

_____

_____

_____

_____

Compare and contrast all three occupations. (B)

_____

_____

_____

_____

_____

_____

"Everyone has been made for some particular work, and the desire to do that work has been put inside their heart." ~ Rumi

Think your morning JUICE. After I read this quote my first thought was, "Well, I guess it's always in the last place you look!" For today's journal entry, continue to describe your ideal, dream job and create two steps you can take toward realizing your dreams.

Date: ____/____/____

Continue to describe your ideal, dream job.

_____

_____

_____

_____

_____

_____

Create two steps you can take toward realizing your dreams.

1) _____

_____

_____

_____

2) _____

_____

_____

_____

"Do what you love, and you will never work another day in your life." ~ George Burns

"Where your talents and the needs of the world cross, there lies your vocation." ~ Aristotle

Think your morning JUICE. I put these quotes together because they follow each other in the book. For today's journal entry, read each quote, say how you'll do it, and describe your inspired thoughts and feelings.

Date: ____/____/____

Read each quote, say how you'll do it, and describe your inspired thoughts and feelings.

Quote 1) _____

_____

_____

_____

Quote 2) _____

_____

_____

_____

"I.S.E.E. My Life's Work!" ~ Laurence Boldt

Think your morning JUICE. This heading appears on page 51 of *Zen and the Art of Making a Living* by Laurence Boldt. (See The Recommended Reading List on my website) I.S.E.E. stands for Integrity Service Enjoyment Excellence and are considered key words. For today's journal entry, find a copy of this book and read this referenced page. Then, rewrite each term's description in your own words, add any additional Key Words you feel are missing, and answer each Essential Question. Finally, describe your inspired thoughts and feelings.

Date: _____/_____/_____

Follow the writing prompts:

Rewrite Integrity) _____

_____

Add Key Words) _____

_____

Answer Essential Question) _____

_____

Rewrite Service)_____

_____

Add Key Words) _____

_____

Answer Essential Question) _____

_____

Rewrite Enjoyment) _____

_____

Add Key Words) _____

_____

Answer Essential Question) _____

_____

Rewrite Excellence) _____

_____

Add Key Words) _____

_____

Answer Essential Question) _____

_____

Describe your inspired thoughts and feelings.

_____

_____

_____

_____

"Choice by choice, moment by moment, I build the necklace of my day, stringing together my choices to form artful living." ~ Julia Cameron

Think your morning JUICE. This quote describes a life of productive time management, which leads to an Occupation of, "artful living." As you read the book section, and this quote, recall the power of making conscious choices, and then do what the quote describes. For today's journal entry, write about the results of a few of your best conscious choices.

Date: _____/_____/_____

Write about the results of a few of your best conscious choices.

1) _____

_____

_____

_____

2) _____

_____

_____

_____

3) _____

_____

_____

_____

4) _____

_____

_____

_____

Exercise 12 - A Week's Worth of Spending: Create a Color Coded, Time Occupations, Bar Graph!

Think your morning JUICE. Use this page to continue or redo Exercise 12. Then, when you have completed the exercise, describe your inspired thoughts and feelings.

Date: _____/_____/_____

_____

_____

_____

_____

_____

_____

_____

_____

_____

_____

_____

_____

_____

_____

_____

_____

_____

_____

_____

_____

"Every minute you are angry, you lose sixty seconds of happiness." ~ Ralph Waldo Emerson

Think your morning JUICE. Now you know what you're missing! This quote reminds me of my mother's anecdotal advice. The story goes when she went to college she also worked as a nurse in three New York City hospitals. Her daily commute consisted of riding on several subway trains and buses. So she made the conscious choice to productively use her travel time as designated "worry time." The way it worked was if during the course of her day she felt herself worrying, she'd stop and tell herself she could only worry on the bus or train. If it were an item "not worth worrying about," she'd forget about it entirely. If she remembered, then she'd have something to think about and occupy her mind as she traveled home. This advice works wonderfully! With it in mind, my transportation time has become much more productive. So I suggest you designate worry time into your daily schedule. For today's journal entry, follow this anecdotal advice and describe a few examples of your results. First, describe the item you worried about. (A) And second, explain how having a special, designated worry time helped you process the item and ultimately live a less stressful life. (B)

Date: _____/_____/_____

Describe an item you worried about (A) and explain how having a special, designated, "worry time," helped you process the item and ultimately live a less stressful life (B).

1A)_____

_____

1B)_____

_____

2A)_____

_____

2B)_____

_____

3A)_____

_____

3B)_____

_____

4A)_____

_____

4B)_____

_____

"Know the value of time; snatch, seize, and enjoy every moment of it." ~ Lord Chesterfield

Think your morning JUICE. This quote reminds me to Carpe Diem. (Seize the day!) Today you need to figuratively stop and smell the roses. Give yourself a present gift and take a LAB (Life Appreciation Break). Take a moment to recognize the value of your time and make a poignant promise to extremely enjoy it. For today's journal entry, write about a few favorite, most memorable LABs.

Date: _____/_____/_____

Write about a few favorite, most memorable LABs:

1) _____

_____

_____

_____

2) _____

_____

_____

_____

3) _____

_____

_____

_____

4) _____

_____

_____

_____

"Time is a created thing. To say, 'I don't have time.' is to say, 'I don't want to.'" ~ Lao Tzu

"I want to exercise, but it is not always possible with my profuse sleep schedule."
~ Author Unknown

Think your morning JUICE. I knew these quotes had to go together because the second quote is a comical example of the first quote's point. For today's journal entry, list of a few, new, "I want to do ..." activity ideas. Plan how you are going to create time, to actually do each activity. Describe how you will feel after you have successfully accomplished all your new activity ideas.

Date: ____/____/____

List a few, new, "I want to do ..." activity ideas.

1) _____

2) _____

3) _____

4) _____

Plan how you're going to, "create" time to actually do each activity.

1) _____
_____

2) _____
_____

3) _____
_____

4) _____
_____

Describe how you feel after you've successfully accomplished all your new activity ideas.

_____

_____

_____

_____

"It's preoccupation with possessions, more than anything else, which prevent us from living freely and nobly." ~ Bertrand Russell

"When we live in bliss, there are no insurmountable difficulties. If we miss the bliss, there are no adequate compensations." ~ Author Unknown

"I think the person who takes a job in order to live - that is to say, (only) for the money - has turned themselves into a slave." ~ Joseph Campbell

"To many people spend money they haven't earned, to buy things they don't want, so they can impress people they don't like." ~ Will Rogers

"Words that enlighten your soul are more precious than jewels." ~ Hazrat Inayat Kahn

"If you are going to let the fear of poverty govern your life … your reward will be you will eat, but you will not live fully." ~ George Bernard Shaw

Think your morning JUICE. These six quotes have a common theme. They all address the idea that how you internally feel about how you spend your time, is much more important than how you externally, materialistically spend your money. Do you agree or disagree? For today's journal entry, answer this question and explain your position. Then describe a few examples of how your conclusions apply in your daily life.

Date: ____/____/____

I _____ (agree or disagree). Explain your position.

_____

_____

Describe a few examples of how your conclusions apply in your daily life.

1) _____

_____

2) _____

_____

3) _____

_____

4) _____

_____

"Sensible people get paid to play." ~ Alan Watts

Think your morning JUICE. As a past, pre-6th grade, Child-Care Teacher, I had to include this quote. Because it was literately part of my job description to play games, do arts and crafts, and produce and perform dramatic plays. Honestly I can't think of a more enjoyable and enormously "sensible" job for me to do. And I hope you are equally fortunate and absolutely able to find your own positively "play-full" profession. For today's journal entry, read the quote, consider the concept, and describe your inspired thoughts and feelings.

Date: ____/____/____

Read the quote, consider the concept, and describe your inspired thoughts and feelings.

_____

_____

_____

_____

Exercise 13 - Compose Yourself: Set Your Present-Day Life-Speeds And Create Your Character's Concerto!

Think your morning JUICE. Use this page to continue or redo Exercise 13. Then, when you have completed the exercise, describe your inspired thoughts and feelings.

Date: ____/____/____

_____

_____

_____

_____

_____

_____

_____

_____

_____

_____

_____

_____

_____

_____

_____

_____

"Affirmations are prescriptions for certain aspects of yourself you want to change."
~ Jerry Frankhauser

"An affirmation is a strong, positive statement, something (you want to change) is already (changed.)" ~ Shakti Gawain

Think your morning JUICE. The ABCs of a Successful Relationship says, "be accountable to your affirmations." And in Chapter 1, you made a list of self-character traits you wanted to change. Now it's time to say how you feel you're doing. For today's journal entry, answer this question, "How are you progressing in your self-help process?" Evaluate yourself on a scale from 1-10 and explain your answer. ("1" is you are the same person when you started only now you're a little bit older and "10" is you couldn't be more satisfied with your progress.)

Date: ____/____/____

On a scale from 1-10, how are you progressing in your self-help process? I'm a _____.
Explain your answer.

_____

_____

_____

_____

"What ultimately holds true is the better a woman's self-esteem, the more likely she is to find a satisfying relationship - and the more she likes her looks, no matter how close or how far away they are to or from the beauty ideal, the better her self-esteem is likely to be." ~ Carolyn Hillman

Think your morning JUICE. Do you agree or disagree? For today's journal entry, answer the question and explain your position. Be specific how your gender influences your answer.

Date: ____/____/____

I _____ (agree or disagree). Explain your position.

_____

_____

_____

_____

"We make a living by what we get, but we can make a life by what we give."
~ Winston Churchill

Think your morning JUICE. Most people associate the phrase "making a living" with receiving a monetary income. But I am using this quote here to show how it applies to relationships. In unbalanced relationships, one side gives more than they get. This doesn't feel secure or healthy. In a balanced relationship, everyone gives as good as they get. These relationships are vital in value, have a higher degree of self-satisfaction in how everyone's "making a living," there's a greater feeling of enjoyment, and there's an extremely enhanced quality of life for everyone involved and invested. For today's journal entry read the quote and describe a few relationships. Label them "unbalanced" or "balanced." Write why you see them this way.

Date: ____/____/____

Describe a few relationships. Label them "unbalanced" or "balanced." Write why.

1) _____

_____

_____

_____

2) _____

_____

_____

_____

3) _____

_____

_____

_____

4) _____

_____

_____

_____

Describe why it is so important to be generous in a relationship and write about how you bring balance to your best.

_____

_____

_____

_____

_____

_____

"A man has to live with himself, and he should see to it that he always has good company." ~ Charles Evans Hughes

Think your morning JUICE. This quote inspires integrity. I read it and I recall an assertion made by countless coaches and sports analysts. They say, "It's only a foul or penalty, if you get caught." I think this is an alarming message for athletes, especially young ones. And to make matters worse, when it's heard on TV the sub-text is: maybe some real-life criminal actions are also alright, as long as you don't get caught. I hope we all know this is a very alarming message, for everyone! For today's journal entry, read the quote and describe your inspired thoughts and feelings. Then explain why integrity is important in sports, society, and especially in relationships.

Date: ____/____/____

Read the quote and describe your inspired thoughts and feelings.

_____

_____

_____

_____

Explain why integrity is important in sports, society, and especially in relationships.

_____

_____

_____

_____

"At the height of laughter, the universe is flung into a kaleidoscope of possibilities."
~ Jean Huston

"Listen, or thy tongue will make thee deaf." ~ Native American Proverb

"The first duty of love is to listen." ~ Paul Tillich

"Life is our greatest possession and love its greatest affirmation!" ~ Leo Buscaglia

"Let It Be." & "Love. Love. Love. All you need is love." ~ The Beatles

Andrewism: What Are You Thinking?

A Couple Of Co-Eds Rest Quietly, Under A Wise-Old-Willow.
Their Beautiful Backdrop Is A Picturesque, Paradise, Public Park.
The Air Is Fresh, Clean, & Filled, With Peaceful, Positive, Teasing Tension.
It Is A Magical-Memory-Moment Just Waiting To Happen.
Then, With A Brief Breeze, Life Is Breathed Into The Scene.
Out Of The Corner Of His Eye, He Sees Her Unmistakable, Only In Our World Famous,
Magically Magnetic, Mysterious & Mischievous, Sexy & Silly, Oh So Special, Smile!
She Calmly Sits, Slowly Eating A Cup-Coned-Super-Sundae, His Treat.
The Warm Summer Sun, Is Simply An Extra Extension, Of Her Ever Present,
Love-Light, Luminescence.
                    (He Asks The Quintessential Question:) "So, What Do You Want To Do Now?"
Inside He Silently Hopes, That She Will Once Again, Play Along, & Participate.
After All, This Is Just One Of Their Countless & Priceless, Daily, Little, Lover's Games.
Of Course, She Is Copiously Co-Operative.
In One, Graceful, Sensual, Smooth, Motion, She Looks Up Into His Eyes, & She Says Her Line.

179

Then, After A Magnificently Milked Moment Of Fantastically Feigned, False Innocence,
She Swallows A Spoonful Of, De-Licious, De-Lightful, De-Lectable, De-Lovely, De-Decadence.

(She Softly Says:) "Oh, I Don't Know. What Do You Want To Do?"

Her Youthful, Pink, Blush Filled Face, Is Once Again, Occupied, With An Orgasmic, Taste:
Choco-Coffee Ice Cream, Caramel, Marshmallow, Hot-Fudge, & COOL-WHIP!
She Has Effortlessly, Become,
Peaceful, Calm, & Sinfully Still.

(He Wantonly Whispers:) "What Are You Thinking?"

Her Sensuous Smile, Quickly Brightens, Beyond Belief.
It Turns On Into An Extremely Excited, Grateful, & Gracious Grin.
Her Bottom Lip Is Being Bit Ever So Slightly.
Her Royal Radiance, Is Only Matched, By Her Now Deepened, Red-Rose Blush.
This Time A Spoonful Of, Syrup-Swirl, & A Maraschino Cherry,
Barely Get Into Her Mouth.

(She Softly Says:) "Oh, Nothing,"

She Suppresses A Small, Girlish, Giggle, &,
She Tosses A Strand Of Long, Soft, Hair,
Out Of Her Sparkling, Star-Light-Bright,
Exhilarated & Elated, Eyes.

(She Softly Says:) "Why Do You Ask?"

She Pauses Just Long Enough For Him To Wake Up From His Delirious, Devine, Daydream,
Gather His Wits About Him, & Vainly Try To Formulate, A Simple, Playful, False, Answer.
Of Course, His Previously Preoccupied Mind, Is Unable, & For That Matter, Unwilling,
To Do Anything, But Silently, & Pleasantly, Visualize His Original, True, Answer.
This Time, Just As It Is Every Time, She Lets Him Off The Hook, Easy.
She Leans Forward, Interlocks Their Eyes, & She Smiles From Deep Inside Their Day-Dream.
At This Magical-Memory-Moment's Mountain Summit, She Reaches Across,
The Small Space, Between Their Bodies, &, She Touches His Hand.
The Pause Has Become, Pregnant.
So, She Plays The Final, Q. & A. Game Card.

(She Softly, Wantonly Whispers:) "What Are You Thinking? Hmmm?"

When Two Hearts, & Two Minds,

LOVE, & They Clearly Create,
Plentiful Passion & One Whole Soul:
This Is The Best Of All Possible Worlds!

Andrewism: Question: What's The Best Thing To Be? Answer: A Beheld!

Question: "What Do You Want To Be?"
     Internal Thought: "Beauty Is In The Eye Of The Beholder."
Answer: "I Want To Be A Be-Hold-Her."
     Internal Thought: "I Want To Be A Be-Held-By-Her."
Question: "What Do You Call Couples Of This Caliber?"
     Internal Thought: "The Answer Is Obvious."
Answer: "They Are The Best Of All Possible Worlds!"
     Internal Thought: "They Are Be-Helds!"

Think your morning JUICE. These six quotes and two *Andrewism* poetry pieces have a common theme of L words. They're laughter, listen, let (It Be) (or as I detailed in Chapter 3, let things go) and most important, love. For today's journal entry, read the quotes and the *Andrewism* poetry pieces and describe your inspired thoughts and feelings. Then, if you're in a "Best Of All Possible Worlds" loving relationship, describe it and explain how it's been beneficial. (Note: This does not have to be a romantic relationship. Family members, BFFs, or even your fabulous, furry friends can be counted in this category.)

Date: _____/_____/_____

Read each quote and describe your inspired thoughts and feelings.

Quote 1) _____

_____

_____

_____

Quote 2) _____

_____

_____

_____

Quote 3) _____

_____

_____

_____

Quote 4) _____

_____

_____

_____

Quote 5) _____

_____

_____

_____

Quote 6) _____

_____

_____

_____

Read each *Andrewism* poetry piece, and describe your inspired thoughts and feelings.

Andrewism 1) _____

_____

_____

_____

_____

Andrewism 2) _____

_____

_____

_____

_____

If you're in a, "Best Of All Possible Worlds," loving relationship, describe it and explain how it's been beneficial.

_____

_____

_____

_____

(Note: At the end of The ABCs Of A Successful Relationship, I urged you to, "A-Z Add Your Own Words." So if you feel there are any words I failed to say, use an Appendix IV: A Blank

Page, and make an alphabetical list of all your additions. Explain why you feel each new word is an important ingredient in every successful relationship.)

"If you've built castles in the air, your work need not be lost; that's where they should be. Now put the foundations under them." ~ Henry David Thoreau

Think your morning JUICE. You've taken several steps toward living a more organized and time-managed life. In short, you've, "built castles in the air." Time-Transitions is the foundation of my four-file system. So put the foundation under your castles. When you focus and pay attention to your Self, Occupations, and Relationships, make sure your Time-Transitions are fluent. For today's journal entry, describe a few examples of how you're productively able to transition from one category to another.

Date: ____/____/____

Describe a few examples of how you're productively able to transition from one category to another.

1) _____

_____

_____

_____

2) _____

_____

_____

_____

3) _____

_____

_____

_____

4) _____

_____

_____

_____

"It don't mean a thing if it ain't got that swing." ~ Duke Ellington

"What we play is life." ~ Louis Armstrong

Think your morning JUICE. These two musicians were experts at producing unique, musical rhythms. So when I read their quotes I knew they'd fit perfectly in this section. I hope they help you compose yourself and discover your Rhythm of Life. For today's journal entry, read the two quotes, and the corresponding book section, and describe your inspired thoughts and feelings.

Date: ____/____/____

Read the two quotes, and the corresponding book section, and describe your inspired thoughts and feelings.

Quote 1) _____

_____

_____

_____

Quote 2) _____

_____

_____

_____

The Book Section) _____

_____

_____

_____

_____

_____

_____

_____

_____

_____

_____

Lonely vs. Alone

"We are all in this alone." ~ Lily Tomlin

Think your morning JUICE. I love this quote. It's funny and it perfectly illustrates the main concept from the corresponding book section. (Even if you're alone in a room you're never alone on the planet.) So when you're feeling lonely, don't just sit and suffer in the feeling. Make a conscious choice to, as the slogan says, "Reach out and touch someone." Or change your negative, lonely feelings into positive, peaceful, energy, which you can use in productive solo-time. For today's journal entry, write about a time when you made this conscious choice. Explain what you did and describe how it helped you.

Date: ____/____/____

Write about a time when you made this conscious choice. Explain what you did and describe how it helped you.

_____

_____

_____

_____

_____

_____

Lifetime Role Models: MAGIC and Sail the Seven Cs!

Andrewism: Buried Treasure!

Birth: Here Is Where, The Search Starts & The Journey Begins
          We Travel Through Time,   Looking For,
                                        True Friends,
                                        True Love,
        And   Our   True Self!

Life: Here Is Where, We Fight The Good Fight, & Overcome Our Obstacles.
          We Arrive At Present Points, Meeting Our,
                                      Most-Valuable-Of-All-Priceless-Possessions,
                                      Buried Treasure,
        And   Our   Lifetime-Love-A-Lots!

Think your morning JUICE. "True Friends, True Love, And Our True [Inner-Highest] Self!" Some people figuratively sail the seven seas and search their whole lives for buried treasure. So, if you ever suspect you've found it, MAGICally make it yours. For today's journal entry read the *Andrewism* poetry piece and describe your inspired thoughts and feelings. Then write about a few of your top MVPs (Most Valuable Persons), self-discovered, priceless, buried treasures.

Date: ____/____/____

Read the *Andrewism* poetry piece, and describe your inspired thoughts and feelings.

_____

_____

_____

_____

Write about a few of your MVPs, self-discovered, priceless, buried treasures.

1) _____

_____

_____

_____

2) _____

_____

_____

_____

3) _____

_____

_____

_____

4) _____

_____

_____

_____

"Creativity is really the structuring of magic." ~ Ann Kent Rush

Think your morning JUICE. This quote restates the concept of MAGIC (Make A Good, Intelligent Choice)! The paradigm in the book is you are learning How to Dramatically Build, (create,) Your Character! So make your conscious, character choices as Good as possible. For today's journal entry, write about a few examples of how you are being creative by smartly, "structuring" your MAGICs.

Date: ____/____/____

Write about a few examples of how you're being creative by smartly, "structuring" your MAGICs.

1) _____

_____

_____

_____

2) _____

_____

_____

_____

3) _____

_____

_____

_____

4) _____

_____

_____

_____

"Moods are contagious. So surround yourself with upbeat, optimistic cast members."
~ Lena Nozizwe

"Nothing is so contagious as an example." ~ François de La Rochefoucauld

Think your morning JUICE. I put these quotes together because they both use "contagious." The word usually has a negative connotation, as in a contagious disease. But in this section, you are Collecting Cool Companions (and you're encouraged to) Consciously Choose them with Clear Criteria! So the "upbeat, optimistic cast members" which you "surround yourself" with are leading you by example, and they are "contagious" with a positive connotation. For today's journal entry, read the quotes, consider the concept, and describe your inspired thoughts and feelings.

Date: _____/_____/_____

Read the quotes, consider the concept, and describe your inspired thoughts and feelings.

Quote 1) _____

_____

_____

_____

Quote 2) _____

_____

_____

_____

Concept) _____

_____

_____

_____

"You should explain the concept of death, very carefully to your children. This will make the action of threatening them with it, a whole lot more effective." ~ P.J. O'Rourke

Think your morning JUICE. This quote is for all adults who want to be lifetime role models for their children. Because seriously, when it comes time to deal with real, life-threatening issues, (i.e., drugs, alcohol, drunk driving, STDs, gangs, guns, violence, etc.) children really do need to understand how dead is dead! In real life, there is no video game replay, reset button, or life extension do-overs! For today's journal entry, read the quote, consider the concept, and describe your inspired thoughts and feelings.

Date: _____/_____/_____

Read the quote, consider the concept, and describe your inspired thoughts and feelings.

_____

_____

_____

_____

_____

_____

"No one can let you down if you haven't been leaning on someone. So if you are going to rely on, or solicit support, from someone, make sure they are of good character and strong foundation." ~ Andrew S. Taylor

Here is a perfect place to put your divine dedication to your tip-top, special someone.

_____

_____

Think your morning JUICE. For today's journal entry, write about a few, really reliable, "I know I can count on…" characters. Describe how you solicit their support, and explain why you feel they are of good character and strong foundation. Then look at the next photograph and describe your inspired thoughts and feelings.

Date: ____/____/____

Follow the writing prompts.

1) _____

_____

_____

_____

2) _____

_____

_____

_____

3) _____

_____

_____

_____

4) _____

_____

_____

_____

Look at the next photographs and describe your inspired thoughts and feelings.

_____

_____

_____

_____

_____

"If people knew how hard I worked, practiced, trained, or studied, to get my mastery, it wouldn't seem so miraculous." ~ Michelangelo

Think your morning JUICE. Lifetime role models can, "make it look easy." Remember, looks can be deceiving. And you should also know ...

"If it was easy, everyone would do it. Hard is what makes it great."
~ Tom Hanks as Jimmy Dugan

Think your morning JUICE. For today's journal entry, read the quotes, consider the concepts, and describe your inspired thoughts and feelings.

Date: ____/____/____

Read the quotes, consider the concepts, and describe your inspired thoughts and feelings.

Quote 1 and 2) _____

_____

_____

_____

Concept Comments)

_____

_____

_____

_____

_____

_____

"Tell me with whom you go, and I will tell you what you do." ~ William Blake

Think your morning JUICE. After I read this quote I thought, *Make sure the company you keep presents a positive picture.* And *When you Collect Cool Companions, make sure one of your Clear Criteria for keeping them as company, is they accurately represent you.* For today's journal entry, answer the questions, "Does the company I keep, precisely represent me?" And/Or, "Does the company I keep, positively present me?" If, "No." how are you going to change? If, "Yes." explain how your company matches you.

Date: ____/____/____

Answer the writing prompt questions. No____. Yes____.

If, "No." how are you going to do to change? If, "Yes." explain how your company matches you.

_____

_____

_____

_____

_____

_____

"If you want to soar with eagles, don't walk around with turkeys." ~ Bumper Sticker

Think your morning JUICE. This is a classic bumper sticker. And you might have seen it on a few other items (i.e., T-shirts, coffee mugs, posters, etc.). For today's journal entry, determine what kind of company you keep. If you are soaring with the eagles, continue keeping their company. But, if you are walking around with a bunch of turkeys, determine how you are going to change. Create a four, flap-by-flap flight plan, and facilitate flying with those finely feathered freedom fowls! Finally, describe your inspired thoughts and feelings.

Date: _____/_____/_____

I'm _____ with the _____. If your answer is, "I'm walking with the turkeys," crate a flap-by-flap flight plan, and facilitate flying with the other, finely feathered freedom fowls! Unfurl your four-flap-by-flap flight plan.

Flap 1) _____

_____

_____

Flap 2) _____

_____

_____

Flap 3) _____

_____

_____

_____

Flap 4) _____

_____

_____

_____

Finally, describe your inspired thoughts and feelings.

_____

_____

_____

_____

Exercise 14 - Discover Who's Been Your Past-to-Present LRMs (Lifetime Role Models) and Determine Your Clear Criteria to be a Future LRM

Think your morning JUICE. Use this page to continue or redo Exercise 14. Then, when you have completed the exercise, describe your inspired thoughts and feelings.

Date: _____/_____/_____

_____

_____

_____

_____

_____

_____

_____

_____

_____

_____

_____

_____

_____

_____

_____

_____

_____

_____

_____

_____

Exercise 15 - Lifetime Role Models: Draw Your Constellations of Characters

Think your morning JUICE. Use this page to continue or redo Exercise 15. Then, when you have completed the exercise, describe your inspired thoughts and feelings.

Date: _____ / _____ / _____

_____

_____

_____

_____

_____

_____

_____
_____
_____
_____
_____
_____
_____
_____
_____
_____
_____
_____
_____
_____

Set Your (Mind's) Set: It Takes All Kinds to Make a World!

"We are what we think. All we are arises with our thoughts. With our thoughts we make the world. Those who seek enlightenment take it upon themselves to dictate their terms to their own mind. Then, they proceed with strong determination." ~ Buddha

Think your morning JUICE. I like to modify this to "strong, confident and committed determination" because those words are extremely important ingredients if you want to successfully set your (mind's) set. For today's journal entry, read the book section and this quote and describe your inspired thoughts and feelings.

Date: ____/____/____

Read the book section and this quote and describe your inspired thoughts and feelings.

_____
_____
_____
_____
_____

"I've made my own world and it's a much better world than I ever saw outside." ~ Louise Nevelson

Think your morning JUICE. I like this quote for two reasons. First, it's a perfect example of someone creating her own reality. Second, I think it's interesting to see a sculptor who creates external and physical works of art, create, and actually prefer, her own internal and mental view of the world. For today's journal entry, describe how you uniquely view your world, both externally and internally.

Date: ____/____/____

Describe how you uniquely view your world, both externally and internally..

_____

_____

_____

_____

_____

_____

"Painting is an attempt to come to terms with life. There are as many solutions as there are human beings." ~ George Tooker

Think your morning JUICE. I like this quote for its use of the word "solutions." I think it applies not just to painting, but to art in general and religion too. How someone, "come(s) to terms with life," and solves life's mysteries, in their mind, is as unique as the individual human. For today's journal entry, choose two more of your PIES (Physical Intellectual Emotional Spiritual), character traits from Chapter 1 (*), and explain how they contribute to your unique view of your world. (**)

Date: ____/____/____

Follow the writing prompts.

Character Trait 1) _____

_____

_____

Character Trait 2) _____

_____

_____

_____

Andrewism: Birds

Black Birds—White Birds
Both Birds—The Best Of All Birds
Red Birds—Orange Birds—Yellow Birds—Green Birds
Blue Birds—Indigo Birds—Violet Birds—Rainbow Birds
Big Birds—Small Birds
Birds Can Be Most Anything
Birds Of Flight—Birds Of Fowl—Birds That Swim—Birds That Scowl
Birds Of Fantasy—Birds That Are Extinct—Birds That Make You Stop And Think
Birds That Shine—Birds That Only Come Around From Time To Time
Birds From Here—Birds From There
Birds Are Everywhere—And So Are Thine

Think your morning JUICE. This *Andrewism* poetry piece, is one of my solutions when I consider the concept of multiculturalism. For today's journal entry, read the *Andrewism* poetry piece, and describe your inspired thoughts and feelings. Then, if you're so inclined, write your own concept solution, poetry piece.

Date: ____/____/____

Read the *Andrewism* poetry piece, and describe your inspired thoughts and feelings.

_____

_____

_____

_____

If you're so inclined, write your own concept solution, poetry piece.

Title:_____

_____
_____
_____
_____
_____
_____
_____
_____
_____
_____
_____

Post View

"I know of no more encouraging fact, than the undeniable ability of a human being to elevate his (or her) life, through conscious choices and purposeful endeavors."
~ Henry David Thoreau

Think your morning JUICE. For today's journal entry, review a few favorite concepts from Chapter 2's making, "conscious choices" through the end of Chapter 4 and continue to describe your inspired thoughts and feelings. Then read about, "purposeful endeavors" and continue our journey in Chapter 5: The Heart Of Your Art!

Date: ____/____/____

Review a few favorite concepts from Chapter 2's making, "conscious choices," through

the end of Chapter 4, and continue to describe your inspired thoughts and feelings.

Chapter 2:

1) _____

_____

_____

_____

2) _____

_____

_____

_____

3) _____

_____

_____

_____

4) _____

_____

_____

_____

Chapter 3:

1) _____

_____

_____

_____

2) _____

_____

_____

_____

3) _____

_____

_____

_____

4) _____

_____

_____

_____

Chapter 4:

1) _____

_____

_____

_____

2) _____

_____

_____

_____

3) _____

_____

_____

_____

4) _____

_____

_____

_____

Extra Expressings and Thoughtful Thinkings: Positivity Paragraphs

Hello! Here are key questions for you all!
What & When will be the next, new, normal?
Well the caregivers, & the life supporters all,
are now deemed, to be essential for us all!
So I say, forevermore, & from-now-on-today,
stay, this course, & know it to be true for you!
Now you know what & who is essential to you!
Everyday simply show, to those needed by you,
HOW VERY MUCH, SO LOVE THEM YOU DO!

Write your inspired thoughts and feelings.
_____
_____
_____
_____
_____
_____
_____
_____

WOW! Much more than mind-heart felt feeling!
SAY IT: To One Who Inspires You Every-Day!
SAY IT: To One Who Needs To Hear It Today!
SAY IT: To One Who Never Hears It Enough!
SAY IT: To One Who Says It To Only Others!
SAY IT: To One Who Needs To Feel It In Self!
SAY IT: To One Who Lives It Extreme-Example!
SAY IT: To One Who Defines The Term DAY-LY!
SAY IT: & KNOW IT: As Your MIRROR-ME-YOU!

Write your inspired thoughts and feelings.
_____
_____
_____
_____
_____
_____
_____
_____

There's a lot of ambiguity in our daily times!
So I see open occasions to give gifts of mines!
Here are simple sentences & great guidances!
Take great care of you! As with others you do!
So show great kindness! As you do your best!
In illness, go home, get rest, in your nice nest!
In health, give thanks, you passed your test!
In life, avoid all apathy, & cooperatively care!
In love, start with self! Then soul-full-ly share!

Write your inspired thoughts and feelings.
_____
_____
_____
_____
_____
_____
_____
_____

To Do My Best-Self: 10 Demand-ments: I WILL!
1] balance others-care & self-care! 2] do 100%
integrity match outside & inside self! 3] make
time most valuable possession! 4] consistently
choose a code of kindness! 5] always adjust my
attitude to embrace my empowerment! 6] see
success as a joy-full journey! 7] hug & behold
beholds, whole-heartedly! 8] LIVE A PURPOSE-
FULL, 9] PASSION-FULL, 10] LOVE-FULL LIFE!

Write your inspired thoughts and feelings.
_____
_____
_____
_____
_____
_____
_____
_____

TODAY'S-THINGS-TO-DO: [1-14 ALL CHECK!]
1] Wake-To-Wonder-Full! 2] Do All Day-Dreams!
3] See-What-Seems! 4] Learn! By All Means!
5] Forge A Friendship! 6] Set All Your Sails!
7] Persist To Your Purpose! 8] Don't Ever Quit!
9] Feed Your Soul's Hunger! 10] ONE Life Is It!
11] Take Aliving Actions! 12] Make Memories!
13] Today: Acknowledge-Appreciate All Family!
14] Today: LIVE-WHOLE-HEARTEDLY-IN-LOVE!

Write your inspired thoughts and feelings.
_____
_____
_____
_____
_____
_____
_____
_____

CREATE YOUR FATE: Prepare Positive Plans!
Each & Every Day, CHOOSE YOUR OWN WAY!
Consciously Live Life! DO Productive Purpose!
Each & Every Moment, Make It Meaning-Full!
Clear Your Own Path! Proceed With Passion!
Each & Every Week, Stay The Course Strong!
Connect ALL Points Of Perfect Potential! AND
Each & Every Month, Year, & ALL LIFETIME,
Construct Your Character As ACCOUNTABLE!

Write your inspired thoughts and feelings.
_____
_____
_____
_____
_____
_____
_____
_____

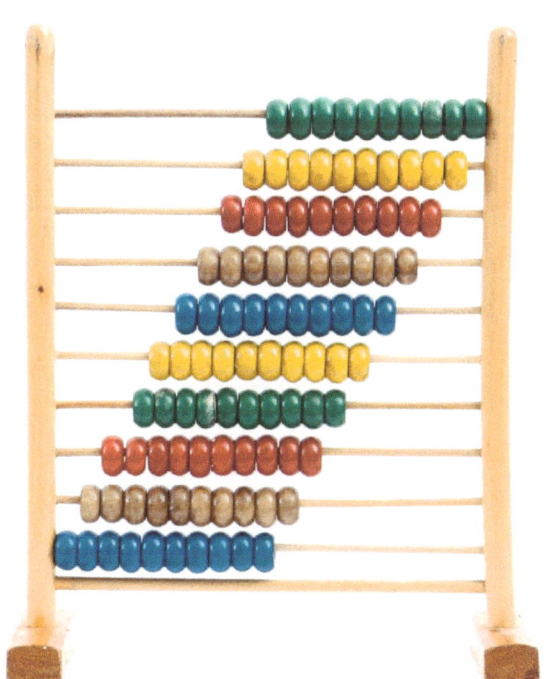

CHAPTER 5:
THE HEART OF YOUR ART!

Preview

"Always bear in mind, your belief in yourself and your resolution to succeed are infinitely more important, than all other single character traits." ~ Abraham Lincoln

Think your morning JUICE. Same as in Chapter 1, ask yourself a few internal character trait questions. Do you believe in you? Do you have a negative or positive attitude? Do you have a weak or strong resolution to succeed? Are you persistent to your purpose? For today's journal entry, write your answers and explain your position.

Date: ____/____/____

Do you believe in you? No____. Yes____.

_____

Do you have a negative or positive attitude? Negative_____. Positive_____.

_____

Do you have a weak or strong resolution to succeed? Weak_____. Strong_____.

_____

Are you persistent to your purpose? No_____. Yes_____.

_____

Attitude and Passion: Eliminate Forecasting FEAR! Do What FUELs You!

"Attitudes for life are as follows:
1) The essence of our being is love.
2) Health is inner peace. Healing is letting go of fear.
3) Giving and receiving are equal.
4) We can let go of the past and the future for they do not exist.
5) Now is the only real time. Each moment is custom made for giving and receiving.
6) We can learn to love others and ourselves by forgiving rather than by judging.
7) We can learn to become love finders rather than faultfinders.

8) We can choose and direct ourselves to be peaceful inside regardless of what's happening outside.
9) We are both students and teachers.
10) We can focus and pay attention to the whole big picture of life, rather than just a few small, sub-sections.
11) Since love is eternal, death should not be feared.
12) We can always perceive others and ourselves as either asking for love or giving love."
~ Author Unknown

Think your morning JUICE. For today's journal entry, write your first impression of each attitude for life, record your overall reaction to the list, and describe any additionally inspired thoughts and feelings.

Date: ____/____/____

Write your first impressions of each attitude for life.

1) _____
_____

2) _____
_____

3) _____
_____

4) _____
_____

5) _____
_____

6) _____
_____

7) _____
_____

8) _____
_____

9) _____

_____

10) _____

_____

11) _____

_____

12) _____

_____

Record your overall reaction to the list.

_____

_____

_____

_____

Describe any additionally inspired thoughts and feelings.

_____

_____

_____

_____

Exercise 16 - Attitude: Is the Universe Friendly?

Think your morning JUICE. Use this page to continue or redo Exercise 16. Then, when you have completed the exercise, describe your inspired thoughts and feelings.

Date: _____ / _____ / _____

_____

_____

_____

_____

_____

_____

_____

_____

_____

_____

"Attitude is the mind's paintbrush. It colors all situations any color you choose!"
~ Author Unknown

Think your morning JUICE. I saw this quote on an art teacher's classroom door. It inspired me to review a few of my past, tough times. I recognized how my present attitude colored my memory of each event. For today's journal entry, do your own recall review and remember a few of your past, tough times. Explain how your present attitude colors your memory of each event.

Date: ____ / ____ / ____

Describe a few past, tough times and explain how your present attitude colors your memory of each event.

1) _____

_____

_____

_____

2) _____

_____

_____

_____

3) _____

_____

_____

_____

4) _____

_____

_____

_____

"The mind ... by itself ... can make a heaven of hell, a hell of heaven." ~ John Milton

"... nothing is either good nor bad, but thinking makes it so." ~ William Shakespeare

"People are about as happy as they make up their minds to be." ~ Abraham Lincoln, The 16th President Of The United States

"The doctors told me I would never walk again. My mother told me I would. So I believed my mother." ~ Wilma Rudolph

Think your morning JUICE. These four quotes deal with the concept of mind over matter. For today's journal entry, read each quote and describe your inspired thoughts and feelings. Then, describe a couple times, when your attitude in the moment, made a noticeable difference in the future.

Date: _____/_____/_____

Read each quote and describe your inspired thoughts and feelings.

Quote 1) _____

_____

_____

_____

Quote 2) _____

_____

_____

_____

Quote 3) _____

_____

_____

_____

Quote 4) _____

_____

_____

_____

Describe a couple times, when your attitude in the moment, made a noticeable difference in the future.

1) _____ ____

_____

_____

_____

2) _____ ____

_____

_____

_____

"One learns best through the heart, not through the eyes or intellect." ~ Mark Twain

"It's only with the heart that one can see rightly; what is essentially invisible to the eye." ~ Antoine De Saint Exupe'ry

"I am only one. I cannot do everything. But I can do something. I will not let what I cannot do interfere with what I can do." ~ Helen Keller

"The blind can only see by looking through rose-colored glasses." ~ Andrew S. Taylor

Think your morning JUICE. These four quotes deal with the concept of your attitude is your internal processor. For today's journal entry, read each quote, and describe your inspired thoughts and feelings. Then describe a couple times when your attitude helped you process and positively learn from an experience.

Date: ____/____/____

Read each quote and describe your inspired thoughts and feelings.

Quote 1) _____

_____

Quote 2) _____

_____

Quote 3) _____

_____

Quote 4) _____

_____

Describe a couple times when your attitude helped you process and positively learn from an experience.

1) _____

_____

_____

_____

2) _____

_____

_____

_____

"Of all base [negative] passions, fear is the most accursed." ~ William Shakespeare

"Our doubts are traitors, and make us lose the good we oft might win by fearing to attempt." ~ William Shakespeare

"You miss 100% of the shots you don't take." ~ Wayne Gretzky

"[FEAR] is interest paid on a debt you may not owe." ~ Peter McWilliams

"I've lived a long life and had many troubles. Most never happened." ~ Mark Twain

"Regret for the things we did can be tempered by time; it is regret for the things we did not do that is inconsolable." ~ Sydney J. Harris

"The fear of rejection is worse than rejection itself." ~ Nora Profit

"Fear is the darkroom where negatives are developed." ~ Michael Pritchard

"If you want a place in the sun, you must leave the shade of the family tree."~ Osage Saying

"We cannot escape fear. We can only transform it into a companion that accompanies us on all of our exciting adventures. ... Take a risk a day. Do one small or bold stroke that will make you feel great once you have done it. Feel the fear and do it anyway." ~ Susan Jeffers

"You gain strength, courage and confidence by every experience in which you really stop to look fear in the face. You are able to say to yourself, 'I have lived through this horror. I can take the next thing that comes along.' You must do the thing you think you cannot do." ~ Eleanor Roosevelt

"I've been absolutely terrified every moment of my life and I've never let it keep me from doing a single thing I wanted to do." ~ Georgia O'Keefe

Think your morning JUICE. (FEARs) These twelve quotes deal with the concepts of forecasting FEARs and how you need to overcome and control your FEARs so they don't disable you from living a successful life. For today's journal entry, read each quotes and describe your inspired thoughts and feelings. Then, describe a couple times, when you were able to overcome, and control, your FEARs, and you successfully accomplished your desired goal.

Date: ____/____/____

Read each quote and describe your inspired thoughts and feelings.

Quote 1) _____

_____

Quote 2) _____

_____

Quote 3) _____

_____

Quote 4) _____

_____

Quote 5) _____

_____

Quote 6) _____

_____

Quote 7) _____

_____

Quote 8) _____

_____

Quote 9) _____

_____

Quote 10) _____

_____

Quote 11) _____

_____

Quote 12) _____

_____

Describe a couple times when you were able to overcome, and control, your FEARs, and you successfully accomplished your desired goal.

1) _____

_____

_____

_____

_____

_____

2) _____

_____

_____

_____

_____

_____

(Note: Georgia O'Keefe is Carole Fletcher's favorite photographer. I highly recommend you find her books at your local library or bookstore. And for further research, I also highly recommend you do an online search with her name as the keyword. The following five pictures were inspired by Georgia O'Keefe's work.)

Look at the photographs and describe your inspired thoughts and feelings.

1) _____
   _____

2) _____
   _____

3) _____
   _____

4) _____
   _____

5) _____
   _____

6) _____
   _____

"When I work, I relax. Doing nothing… makes me tired." ~ Pablo Picasso

"When love and talent work together, expect masterpieces." ~ John Ruskin

"Genius is an affair of energies!" ~ Matthew Arnold

"The real secret of success is passionate enthusiasm." ~ Walter Chrysler

Think your morning JUICE. These four quotes focus on the activities, which FUEL you. And if you don't know what FUELs you, then for today's journal entry answer this question: If you were a shape shifter* who or what would you become and what would you do? Explain your choices. Answering this question will give you a huge hint in your search for, and your ultimate discovery of, the specific activities which FUEL you.

(Note: You actually do have this super-power! Granted your real-life abilities may not manifest themselves in the same way as your favorite cool and colorful comic book, TV, or movie characters do. As you progress through this book and workbook, and as you Dramatically Build Your Character & Live the Life FANTASTIC, you are real-ly shape shifting yourself into a whole new self-helped you. And if you want to see real-life, super-hero-esque examples of this ability, look at people who have lost large amounts of weight, gone through extreme makeovers, or become self-made millionaires.)

Date: _____/_____/_____

If you were a shape shifter who or what would you become and what would you do? Explain your choices.

1) I would become _____ because _____

_____

2) I would become _____ because _____

_____

3) I would become _____ because _____

_____

4) I would become _____ because _____

_____

1) I would do the activity _____ because _____

_____

2) I would do the activity _____ because _____

_____

3) I would do the activity _____ because _____

_____

4) I would do the activity _____ because _____

_____

"You should never doubt that a small group of thoughtful, committed citizens, can change the world. Indeed it's the only thing that ever has." ~ Margaret Mead, Anthropologist

Think your morning JUICE. This quote appears on page 350 in Zen and the Art of Making a Living by Laurence G. Boldt (*See The Recommended Reading List). The page describes The Power Of Team Working and T.E.A.M. is created into an acronym*. (*See the next quote.) (For a complete, detailed explanation of each word, read the page in the book.)

"Together: [A team has] the strength of a common purpose.
Each: Commitment to [the] team motivates each [member] to excel and grow.
Accomplishes: A team is organized for action.
More: [In a team,] the whole is greater than the sum of its parts." ~ Laurence G. Boldt

Think your morning JUICE. For today's journal entry, do the following three writing prompts: First, read both quotes and describe your inspired thoughts and feelings. Second, write about the best team you were ever associated with and explain what made it the best. And third, explain how being associated with this team has inspirationally improved your attitude, and positively changed your life.

Date: ____/____/____

Read both quotes and describe your inspired thoughts and feelings.

Quote 1) _____

_____

_____

_____

Quote 2) _____

_____

_____

_____

Write about the best team you were ever associated with and explain what made it the best.

_____

_____

_____

_____

Explain how being associated with this team has inspirationally improved your attitude, and positively changed your life.

_____

_____

_____

_____

Be Perceptive from Your Perspective! Be Persistent to Your Purpose!

"Imagination is the rudder of the senses." ~ Leonardo Da Vinci

Think your morning JUICE. I begin with this quote because it's consistent with the sailing analogy I've been using throughout the book, and because I like how it infers a real relationship between the senses and our imagination. As I understand it, you are perceptive with your senses and you interpret with your imagination. For today's journal entry, read the quote, consider the concept, and describe your inspired thoughts and feelings.

Date: ____/____/____

Read the quote, consider the concept, and describe your inspired thoughts and feelings.

_____

_____

_____

_____

"Genius in truth means little more than the faculty of perceiving in an un-habitual way."
~ William James

"To revisit old problems and to approach them from new angles requires creative imagination and marks real advances in science." ~ Albert Einstein

Think Your Morning JUICE. These two quotes remind me of my presentation activity. First, I talk about how some sensational and dramatic public speakers give a few fortunate audience members the opportunity to "miraculously" walk barefoot on hot coals without getting burned. Then I say, "I am not one of those speakers. But I am here to give one of you the chance to perform a non-miracle. This is an action, which is commonly considered to be a miracle, but in reality everyone can do it. Everyone can walk on water!" This usually inspires looks of skepticism and disbelief. But I push forward and ask for a volunteer. (If it is available, I make sure the volunteer is named Will, Bill, or Jill and if any of these names aren't available, I ask the volunteer to confidently say, "I will do it!" and I hang a sign around their neck which says, "I WILL!") Then I retrieve a previously prepared, towel-covered, large, deep-dish tray. I tell the audience the tray contains, "real and non-miraculous water," and the volunteer will easily stand and walk on it without any mirrors or magic tricks. And with a little improvised drum roll I ask the volunteer to, "perform the non-miracle." They are easily able to do it because the water is ... ice!

When the moment's passed and I feel the audience understands the underlining perspective point I conclude the activity with a tag-on joke. I say, "So now you know when you want to do something most people perceive to be impossible, it might only be a matter of changing your perspective and you will make it possible. And, always remember, where there is a Will, Bill, Jill, or an, "I WILL!" there's always a way!"

For today's journal entry, read the quote, consider the presentation activity, and describe your inspired thoughts and feelings. Then choose your favorite example of how the impossible became possible. Explain why it is your favorite choice, and describe how the invention or discovery was beneficial for humanity. (For example, it used to be impossible for people to fly. Now it is possible for millions of people to do it everyday. And obviously this holistically helps humanity.) Finally, if you have an idea for a future possibility, describe it as a soon-to-be probability, and explain how you believe your idea will be beneficial for humanity.

Date: ____/____/____

Read the quote, consider the presentation activity, and describe your inspired thoughts and feelings.

_____

_____

_____

_____

_____

_____

Describe your favorite example of how the impossible became possible. (AKA your favorite invention or discovery.)

_____

_____

_____

_____

_____

_____

Explain why the invention or discovery is your favorite choice.

_____

_____

Explain how you believe your idea will be beneficial for humanity.

_____

_____

If you want, do a small, simple drawing of your invention idea in the space below.

"Technology is synonymous with tool. Teeth, claws, and fire were once very high-tech."
~ Tom Clancy

Think your morning JUICE. I include this quote because it puts human history in perspective. On the one hand, it shows how far we've come. On the other hand, it begs the question, "Which of our present-day, high-tech tools, will someday be our future's, archaic antiques?" Another question is, "How long will it take for our high-tech conveniences to become outdated?" For today's journal entry, read the quote, consider the concept, answer the questions, and describe your inspired thoughts and feelings.

Date: ____/____/____

Read the quote, consider the concept, answer the questions, and describe your inspired thoughts and feelings.

_____

_____

_____

_____

Andrewism: A Cloud & The Eye Of The Beholder

This Is A Definition Of A Cloud According To An Adult:
    A Cloud Is A Visual Accumulation Of Water Vapor.
        This Is A Point Of Interest For Any Weather Reporter:
            The Size, Shape, And Altitude Of Clouds
                Can Help A Person Predict Possible Wet Weather.
These Are A Few Descriptions Of A Cloud According To A Child:
It's A White Bunny's Cottontail!
    It's A White Dragon's Spiny Sail!
        It's A White Puppy Dog And A White Puddy Cat, Playing In A Pail!
            It's A White… Any-Thing… And The Sky's The Limit.
This Is What I Wonder: When Does Our Point Of View Change?
    When Do Our Beholders' Eyes Establish A Factual Focus?
    When Do Our Child's Eyes Change To An Adult's Eyes?
    Is There One Thunderstorm Event Where Torrents Of Harsh Reality Rain Down
        And Drown Out Our Internal Innocence?
    Are Our Childhood Abilities Gradually Cast Over With The Oncoming Of Our
        Overcast Years?
    Is There An Alternative?
        Can The Beholder Consciously Choose?
        Can We Develop Our Child's Eyes, And Our Adult's Eyes, Together?
This Is What I Believe: Yes! Yes We Can!
    This Is What I Know To Be True!
    This Is What I Do:
    I Keep Both Eyes Open,
    And I Successfully Saturate My Life, With Enlightening Out- And In-sight!
This Is What I Advise: Any Young Or Experienced Adult Should Cautiously Counsel Children To,
    "Take Shelter From The Storm."
    And, "Take An Umbrella. It's Better To Be Safe Than Sorry."
    And Any Youth Or Experienced Adult Should Also Take This Same Advice To Heart,
    And As Much As Possible, "Sing And Dance In The Rain."
    And, "Play In All The Puddles You Can Find."
This Is What I Wish:
    On All Your Cloudy Days, May You Always See Clearly And Positively.
        And With Undoubting Patience, Understanding, And Both Eyes Open,
            May You Behold, Embrace, And Enjoy All The Rainbows And Sunrays,
                Which Will Soon Break Through The Clouds And Illuminate Your Life!

Think your morning JUICE. For today's journal entry, read the *Andrewism* poetry piece and describe your inspired thoughts and feelings. Then, if you're so inclined, write your own perspective dependent poetry piece.

Date: ____/____/____

Read the *Andrewism* poetry piece and describe your inspired thoughts and feelings.

_____

_____

_____

_____

If you're so inclined, write your own perspective dependent poetry piece.

Title:_____

_____

_____

_____

_____

_____

_____

_____

_____

_____

_____

_____

_____

_____

"When you come to a fork in the road, take it!" ~ Yogi Berra

"Never go to a doctor whose office plants have died." ~ Emma Bombeck

"I used to work in a fire hydrant factory. You couldn't park anywhere near the place."
~ Steven Wright

"I bought some batteries, but they weren't included." ~ Steven Wright

"I was walking down the street wearing glasses when the prescription ran out."
~ Steven Wright

"When you shoot a mime, do you need to use a silencer?" ~ Steven Wright

"My theory of evolution is that Darwin was adopted." ~ Steven Wright

"I never forget a face, but in your case I'll make an exception." ~ Groucho Marx

"The guy who invented the wheel was an idiot. The guy who invented the other three, he was a genius!" ~ Sid Ceasar

"Weather forecast for tonight: Dark!" ~ George Carlin

"Last night I discovered a new form of oral contraception. I asked a girl to go to bed with me. She said no." ~ Woody Allen

"Condoms aren't completely safe. A friend of mine was wearing one and he got hit by a bus." ~ Bob Rubin

Think your morning JUICE. These are twelve of my favorite comedic quotes. Their sources are extremely perceptive people with highly developed comic perspectives. For today's journal entry, write your top twelve favorite comic quotes. Cite each quote's source and tell the story of the time when you heard it first.

Date: ____/____/____

Quote 1/Source/First time heard) _____

_____

_____

_____

_____

_____

Quote 2/Source/First time heard) _____

_____

_____

_____

_____

_____

Quote 3/Source/First time heard) _____

_____

_____

_____

_____

_____

Quote 4/Source/First time heard) _____

_____

_____

_____

_____

_____

Quote 5/Source/First time heard) _____

_____

_____

_____

_____

_____

Quote 6/Source/First time heard) _____

_____

_____

_____

_____

Quote 7/Source/First time heard) _____

_____

_____

_____

Quote 8/Source/First time heard) _____

_____

_____

_____

_____

_____

Quote 9/Source/First time heard) _____

_____

_____

_____

_____

_____

Quote 10/Source/First time heard) _____

_____

_____

_____

_____

_____

Quote 11/Source/First time heard) _____

_____

_____

_____

_____

_____

Quote 12/Source/First time heard) _____

_____

_____

_____

_____

_____

"Life's like a dogsled team. If you're not the lead dog, the scenery never changes."
~ Lewis Gizzard

Think your morning JUICE. I hope this quote gives you a certain comic perspective, which encourages you to be the lead-er in the play of your life. Because if you only concede to be a follower, you might miss life's most beautiful scenery. For today's journal entry, read the quote, look at the photograph and describe your inspired thoughts and feelings.

Date: ____/____/____

Read the quote, look at the photograph, and describe your inspired thoughts and feelings.

_____

_____

_____

_____

"Nothing great has ever been achieved except by those who dared to believe something inside them was superior to their present circumstances." ~ Bruce Barton

"People are always blaming their circumstances on what they are or where they are from. I don't believe this is true. The people who truly succeed in this world, are the people who get up and look for the circumstances they want. If they can't find them, they change their perspective, and they create the circumstances they want, on their own." ~ George Bernard Shaw

"Some of us have great runways already built for us. If you have one, take off! But if you don't have one, realize it is your responsibility to grab a shovel and build one for yourself, and (maybe more importantly,) for all those who will follow after you." ~ Amelia Earhart

"There are three kinds of people: the ones who wonder what happened, the ones who watch what happens, and those who make things happen." ~ Author Unknown

Think your morning JUICE. These four quotes revisit the concept how you can either be a re-acting follower or an acting lead-er. (See Chapter 2.) Once again I encourage you to be a human doing and to be proactive. Be the acting lead-er of your character construction project. For today's journal entry, read the quotes, consider the concept advice, and describe your inspired thoughts and feelings.

Date: _____ / _____ / _____

Read each quote and describe your inspired thoughts and feelings.

Quote 1) _____

_____

Quote 2) _____

_____

Quote 3) _____

_____

Quote 4) _____

_____

Concept Comments) _____

_____

_____

_____

_____

_____

"[Q: How do I get to be real? A: To be real ...] It doesn't happen all at once. ... You become. It takes a very long time." ~ Margery Williams, *The Velveteen Rabbit*

"It takes a long time to bring excellence to maturity." ~ Publilus Syrus

Think your morning JUICE. These two quotes deal with the concept of there's no such thing as an overnight success. (Or at least it is extremely rare. For example, Mike Myers got a job with Second City two hours after his high school final exam!) For today's journal entry, read the quotes, consider the concept, and describe your inspired thoughts and feelings.

Date: ____/____/____

Read the quotes, consider the concept, and describe your inspired thoughts and feelings.

_____

_____

_____

_____

_____

_____

"There is one quality, one must possess, to win and to be successful, and that is to have definiteness of purpose. This means one must have the clear and specific knowledge of what one wants and a burning desire to be tenaciously persistent to possess it." ~ Napoleon Hill

"My strength lies solely in my tenacity." ~ Louis Pasteur

Think your morning JUICE. Louis Pasteur was a man ahead of his time. In the mid-1800s he theorized how microscopic germs and bacteria were the cause of deadly infections, illnesses, and the spoiling of food. He hypothesized this theory and spent much of his adult life persistently advocating, and finally confirming, the theory. Today he is best remembered for creating the first vaccine for rabies and for demonstrating how to prevent milk from going sour. This process is called pasteurization.

Fortunately, I have seen the results of Pasteur's persistence to purpose first hand. I was studying to be an EMT, and as part of my clinical observation I was given permission to witness quad-abdominal-aorta aneurism surgery. First, the nurse showed me where it was safe to stand. I was told this was outside an established sterile field. As I watched this late-night, lifesaving operation, I saw how every item which was brought into the sterile field was either covered in sterile protection or taken out of its own sterile packaging. After six hours I thought, *If Louis Pasteur could have traveled forward in time, seen this display of standard operating procedure, and then gone back to his own time, I think he would have easily been able to deal with any doubters. Pasteur's work would have been validated right before his very eyes.*

For today's journal entry, read the quotes and story, describe your inspired thoughts and feelings, and, if available, write about an idea you have persistently promoted and you hope to someday prove, produce, and do.

Date: ____/____/____

Read the quotes and story and describe your inspired thoughts and feelings.

Quotes 1 and 2) _____

_____

The story) _____

_____

_____

_____

Write about an idea you have persistently promoted and you hope to someday prove, produce, and do.

_____

_____

_____

_____

"Nothing in the world can take the place of persistence. Talent will not. Nothing is more common than unsuccessful people with talent. Genius will not. Unrewarded genius is almost a proverb. Education will not. The world is full of educated derelicts. Persistence and determination alone are supremely important!" ~ Calvin Coolidge

Think your morning JUICE. I like this quote because it puts persistence in proper perspective and shows why acquiring and developing this, "supremely important" character trait, needs to be your top priority. The quote states persistence is more important than talent, genius, and education, and I whole-heartedly agree! For today's journal entry, read the quote and describe your inspired thoughts and feelings.

Date: _____/_____/_____

Read the quote and describe your inspired thoughts and feelings.

_____

_____

_____

_____

_____

_____

"We don't like their sound, and guitar music is on the way out."
~ A DECCA Records executive rejecting The Beatles

"Falling's part of the game. No matter how good you are, ice is still slippery."
~ Michelle Kwan

"It's not whether you get knocked down; it's whether you get up." ~ Vince Lombardi

"Thousands of people have talent. I might as well congratulate you for having eyes in your head. The one and only thing that counts is: Do you have staying power?" ~ Noel Coward

"You have got to wake up every morning with determination if you are going to go to bed with satisfaction." ~ George Horace Lorimer

"Great works are given birth and performed not by feats of strength (alone), but by consistent perseverance toward the (desired) goal." ~ Samuel Johnson

Think your morning JUICE. These six quotes continue to present the concept of how persistence is paramount in its importance. For today's journal entry, read each quote and describe your inspired thoughts and feelings. Then describe how you are already persistent in pursuing your ambitions. Or explain how you plan to be more persistent in the near future.

Date: _____/_____/_____

Read each quote and describe your inspired thoughts and feelings.

Quote 1) _____

_____

_____

_____

Quote 2) _____

_____

_____

_____

Quote 3) _____

_____

_____

_____

Quote 4) _____

_____

_____

_____

Quote 5) _____

_____

_____

_____

Quote 6) _____

_____

_____

_____

Describe how you are already persistent in pursuing your ambitions. Or, explain how you plan to be more persistent in the near future.

_____

_____

_____

_____

_____

_____

"Make your work to be in keeping with your purpose." ~ Leonardo Da Vinci

"The purpose of life is a life of purpose." ~ Robert Byrne

Think your morning JUICE. The first quote gives good advice and the second quote answers the age-old question, "What is the purpose of life?" For today's journal entry, read each quote and describe your inspired thoughts and feelings. And answer these two questions, "Do you follow the good advice?" (A) and "Do you agree with the purpose of life answer?" (B) Explain your answers.

Date: ____/____/____

Read each quote and describe your inspired thoughts and feelings.

Quote 1) _____

_____

Quote 2) _____

_____

Answer the two questions.

A) No_____. Yes_____. Why? _____

_____

B) I _____ (disagree or agree). Why? _____

_____

"Our true purpose here on Earth is to do good for others. What all the others are here for I don't know." ~ W.H. Auden

"Cats are intended to teach us how not everything in nature has a function or purpose."
~ Garrison Keillor

Think your morning JUICE. These are my last two, comic perspective quotes. (And it occurs to me that when you consider their calm character traits, cats are in fact, by nature, a natural, purring-puss.) But seriously, for today's journal entry continue to write about a couple favorite concepts from the book sections. Give your chosen concepts a title and continue to describe your inspired thoughts and feelings.

Date: ____/____/____

Give your chosen concepts a title and continue to describe your inspired thoughts and feelings.

Concept title) _____

_____

_____

Concept title) _____

_____

_____

Content and Comfortable vs. Happy and Hungry!

Andrewism: Life: Do The Dance!

The Dynamic D.J. Starts The Magical Musicians.
The Gratuitous Groups Grope For Their Platonic Positions.
The Wanton Wallflowers Will Begin To Gather & Grow.
The Single Seeds Of Hope They Beget And Sow.
The Goal Guided Genders Review Their Character Criteria.
The Sexual Subtext Tension Builds To Heightened Hysteria.
The Base Beat Bounces Their Frantic Focus.
The Heat Beaded Bodies Swarm Like Liquid Locus.
The Enchanted Eyes Interlock & Mouthwatering Messages Are Exchanged.
The Tempest Tempo Transitions & The Floor's Plentiful Population Is Changed.
The Slow Song Swayers Contemplate Casual Or Committed Copulation.
The Once Kinetic Congregation Now Rests & It Realizes The Dance's Completion.

Think your morning JUICE. Attending countless high school dances both as a teenage participant and later as an adult chaperone inspired me to write this *Andrewism* poetry piece. If you aren't familiar with it, listen to Leann Womack's song "I Hope You Dance." It reminds you to get your fill to but never lose the hunger inside you. I believe this state of living hungry in your heart is literately vital for all alive human doings. For today's journal entry, read the *Andrewism* poetry piece, complete the statement, "I am hungry for …," explain your choice, and if you are so inclined write your own dance inspired or "I am hungry for (you fill in the blank)" poetry piece.

Date: _____/_____/_____

Read the *Andrewism* poetry piece and describe your inspired thoughts and feelings.

_____

_____

_____

_____

Complete the statement, "I am hungry for _____." Explain your choice.

I feel this way because _____

_____

_____

_____

_____

_____

Write your own dance inspired or, "I am hungry for (you fill in the blank)" poetry piece.

Title:_____

_____

_____

_____

_____

_____

_____

_____

_____

_____

_____

"We act as though comfort and luxury were the real requirements of life, when all we need to be happy is to have something real we can be enthusiastic about." ~ Charles Kingsley

Think your morning JUICE. For today's journal entry, read the quote and describe your inspired thoughts and feelings. Then, answer the question, "What actions would you do if money were no object?" (This is after you have bought all of the "comfort and luxury" items you have always wanted.) List a few of your action choices and describe one. Make sure you show your enthusiasm.

Date: ____/____/____

Read the quote and describe your inspired thoughts and feelings.

_____

_____

_____

_____

Answer the question, "What actions would you do if money were no object?"

1) _____

2) _____

3) _____

4) _____

Describe one action choice. Make sure you show your enthusiasm.

_____

_____

_____

_____

"There are costs and risks to a program of action, but they are far less than the long range costs and risks of comfortable inaction." ~ John F. Kennedy

Think your morning JUICE. For today's journal entry, follow these writing prompts: Choose one aspect of your life where you are simply content and comfortable. Give the aspect a name (1) and explain why it is your first choice. (2) Next, determine a course of action on how you will get out of your comfort zone and list four steps you need to take to achieve your goal. (3) Finally, when you are ultimately successful, describe how it feels to be newly happy and hungry. (4)

Date: ____/____/____

1) The Aspect's Name) _____ 2) It's my first choice because _____

_____

List the steps you need to take to achieve your goal (3).

1) _____

2) _____

3) _____

4) _____

Describe how it feels to be newly happy and hungry (4).

_____

_____

_____

_____

"A musician must make music, an artist must make art, and a writer must write, if they are ever to be at peace with themselves." ~ Abraham Maslow

Think your morning JUICE. When I first read this quote I thought, "True! And artists and musicians must be living a, 'What have I done for myself lately?' life. They can't ever be content. They can't ever sit back on their laurels, relax, and be comfortable with what they've already done." With the book section, I'm making the argument how this concept should apply to everyone who perceives they are on a creative journey of character construction.

In short, as much as possible, everyone should strive to be happy and hungry. For today's journal entry, read the quote, consider the concept, and describe your inspired thoughts and feelings.

_____

_____

_____

_____

"If you want to be happy, set a goal, which commands your thoughts, liberates your energy, and inspires your hope!" ~ Andrew Carnegie

A Jester's Joke & A Total Truth:
Question: How do you get to Carnegie Hall? Answer: Practice!

Post View

"To passionately and persistently work toward a great purpose. … This noble pursuit is larger than ourselves and is the best way to make your life meaningful. When we do this, our self-worth overflows our personal borders, and the memory of our life can ultimately survive our unavoidable death." ~ Will Durant

"When you are inspired by some great purpose, some extraordinary project, all of your thoughts break their bonds. Your mind transcends limitations; your consciousness expands in every direction; and you find yourself in a new, great and wonderful world. Dormant forces, faculties and talents become alive and you discover yourself to be a greater person than you ever dreamed yourself to be." ~ Patanjali

"Our deepest fear is not that we are inadequate. Our deepest fear is that we are powerful beyond measure. It is our light, not our darkness that most frightens us. We ask ourselves, Who am I to be brilliant, gorgeous, talented, and fabulous? Actually, who are you not to be? You are a child of God. Your playing small does not serve the world. There is nothing enlightened about shrinking so that other people will not feel insecure around you. We are all meant to shine, as children do. We were born to make manifest the glory of God that is within us. It is not just in some of us; it is in everyone and as we let our own light shine, we unconsciously give others permission to do the same. As we are liberated from our own fear, our presence automatically liberates others. ~ Marianne Williamson

"When you practice extreme self care, you wrap yourself in an energy that creates miracles in your life and also in the lives of everyone else around you." ~ Shirley Anderson

"Thousands of candles can be lighted from a single candle, and the life of the candle will not be shortened. Happiness is never decreases by being shared." ~ Buddha

"I offer my dreams as a source of love to the world. In their fulfillment I will bring a message of light to all I touch." ~ Sonia Choquette

Think your morning JUICE. These six quotes cover several, major concepts in Chapter 5. For today's journal entry, read each quote and describe your inspired thoughts and feelings. Then, continue to write about a few favorite concepts from Chapter 5. (For identification give each concept a title.) Then, continue our journey in Chapter 6: The Curtain Call!

Date: ____/____/____

Read each quote and describe your inspired thoughts and feelings.

Quote 1) _____

_____

_____

_____

Quote 2) _____

_____

_____

_____

Quote 3) _____

_____

_____

_____

Quote 4) _____

_____

_____

_____

Quote 5) _____

_____

_____

_____

Quote 6) _____

_____

_____

_____

Continue to write about a few favorite concepts from Chapter 5. (For identification give each concept a title.)

Concept title) _____ / _____

_____

_____

_____

_____

_____

Concept title) _____ / _____

_____

_____

_____

_____

_____

Concept title) _____ / _____

_____

_____

_____

_____

_____

Concept title) _____ / _____

_____

_____

_____

_____

_____

Extra Expressings and Thoughtful Thinkings: Positivity Paragraphs

YES-TO-TODAY! NO-Promised-TO-morrow-Time!
YES-TO-(Ter)-Days: Life-Time-Lessons-To-Learn!
YES-TO-LIFE! Your Destiny: Find-&-Full-Fill-It!
YES-TO-QUALITY-TIME! NO-Measure Quantity!
YES-TO-TELL-TRUTH! TO-Self! & TO-All-Souls!
YES-TO-TOTAL-TOLERANCE! TO-All-Humanity!
YES-TO-AN-ATTITUDE-OF-GRATTITUDE! Always!
YES-TO-PERSISTENCE-TO-PURPOSE-FOR-LIFE!
YES-TO-LOVE! For-Friends-Family-&-ALL-Forms!

Write your inspired thoughts and feelings.
_____
_____
_____
_____
_____
_____
_____
_____
_____

HAPPINESS IS: Free-Time On A Time-Less Day!
Simply Thinking! Kindly Knowing What To Say!
Having True Friends! Feeling For Your Family!
Being Someone's Special! Not Only A-You-A-Me!
Healing A Heart! Yours-Mine: Full-For-All-Time!
Making Music & Dance! Never Miss A Chance!
Defining For Yourself: My Definition Success!
Knowing How Fearing Is The Only Real Failing!
LOVING LIFE! DOING HEART-FULL-LY HAPPY!

Write your inspired thoughts and feelings.
_____
_____
_____
_____
_____
_____
_____
_____
_____

TRUTH & REALITY: No Matter What IT IS!
YOU BELIEVING IN IT MAKES IT ALL REAL!
YOU are your consciousness's confirmation!
YOU are your perceptions-present processor!
YOU are your attitude's adamant adjuster!
YOU are your life's most loyal love-a-lot-able!
YOU are your universe's ultimate container!
YOU are your soul's 1st reasonable responder!
YOU are your miracle! Making the most magic!

Write your inspired thoughts and feelings.
_____
_____
_____
_____
_____
_____
_____
_____

This is a paragraph of positive perceptions!
Open Mind & Heart: Eyes see at their best!
Same is also true of how our ears hear!
Beyond smell, sometimes the nose knows!
Your taste is your tangible truth! Live It! &
There is nothing more refreshing, rectifying,
Restoring, repairing, reviving, rejuvenating,
revitalizing, reinvigorating, & regenerating,
than two people touching, with tenderness!

Write your inspired thoughts and feelings.
_____
_____
_____
_____
_____
_____
_____
_____

External is everything all encompassing!
Internal is intangibly infinite! THEY are all!
Einstein said, "Imagination is much more
important than knowledge!" So I say, use it!
AND, … Smartness can be oh so satisfying!
BUT, … Sweetness & Pleasantness can be
OH SO MUCH MORE Positively Productive!
THE KEY IS TO FIND & BE IN BALANCE!
HARMONEY LEADS YOU TO HAPPINESS!

Write your inspired thoughts and feelings.
_____
_____
_____
_____
_____
_____
_____
_____

The Universe is everything real! It is all that is!
The Human Mind is everything *sur*-real! All else!
So embrace, encompass, & empower everything!
Understand *The/Our Universe is a singularity!*
We envision it all in our imaginations! It is ONE!
No individual point is *THE* center! It is boundless!
Only with egocentric eyes, do we see ourselves as
A center! It is absolutely beyond boundaryless!
So now you know! ALL THE UNIVERSE IS YOU!

Write your inspired thoughts and feelings.
_____
_____
_____
_____
_____
_____
_____
_____

Greatness! It is what we all want to achieve!
This is totally true! This is what I do believe!
But then I think, with my usual contemplation!
This is already our state! Our present situation!
You are the greatest you, who will ever be now!
You living you! This is true greatness! Wow!
So keep moving forward! And keep doing you!
With attitudes of gratitude, grow in all you do!
Pass all your tests! & DO TRUE GREATNESS!

Write your inspired thoughts and feelings.
_____
_____
_____
_____
_____
_____
_____
_____

Humanitarian: Should apply 100% HUMANS?
Division-ISMs/Segregations: 100% FOR NONE!
Labels/Definitions: ALL GIVEN BY OTHERS!
Behaviors/Actions: ALL SHOW TRUE SELF!
Character Construction: LIFETIME OF WORK!
Persistence To Purpose: TRUST THE PROCESS!
Attitude Gratitude: THE WAY TO ABUNDANCE!
Mind & Heart: SAFEST HOMES OF FREEDOME!
Your Soul's Success: HEART-FULL HAPPINESS!

Write your inspired thoughts and feelings.
_____
_____
_____
_____
_____
_____
_____
_____

Okay. Now turn the page.

CHAPTER 6:
THE CURTAIN CALL!

Preview

"You have deep within you, the power to fulfill your highest vision of your life. To engage this power you must develop a solid personal relationship with yourself. By doing this, you will tap into a naturally flowing fountain of inner strength that will allow you to take all the necessary actions, which will build your confidence and positive self-esteem. When you learn to stop hiding your power, and (you are able to transpose) FEAR (into courage, and use this positive energy) to your advantage, you will become less attached to what others want for you, and more invested in what you want for yourself. And as this shift occurs, you will naturally begin to lead a more authentic and passionate life." ~ Cheryl Richardson

NOW THAT SOUNDS LIKE A PLAN! **A+** 😊

Think your morning JUICE. This quote continues the theme of the six quotes from Chapter 5's Post View. In Chapter 6: The Curtain Call you will be reading the following book sections: Character Conclusions, Character Continuations, Get GIGSS (Gather In Group Support Systems), Celebrate Family & Friends, and Create Unity & Community. For today's journal entry, describe your first impressions of the six Chapter 6 concepts, read the quote above, look at the photograph below, and describe your inspired thoughts and feelings.

Date: _____/_____/_____

Describe your first impressions of the six Chapter 6 concepts. (For identification, give each concept a title.)

Concept title) _____/_____

_____

_____

_____

_____

_____

Concept title) _____/_____

_____

_____

_____

_____

_____

Concept title) _____/_____

_____

_____

_____

_____

_____

Concept title) _____/_____

_____

_____

_____

_____

_____

Concept title) _____/_____

_____

_____

_____

_____

_____

Concept title) _____/_____

_____

_____

_____

Read the quote above and describe your inspired thoughts and feelings.

Look at the photographs below and describe your inspired thoughts and feelings.

Character Conclusions

"Two roads diverged in a wood, and I - I took the one less traveled by, and that has made all the difference." ~ Robert Frost

Think your morning JUICE. This quote is used in Character Conclusion 5: Take The Road Less Traveled By! For today's journal entry, read each character conclusion and describe your inspired thoughts and feelings. And, if you have thought of your own character conclusions, describe a couple of your best ideas.

Date: _____/_____/_____

Read each character conclusion and describe your inspired thoughts and feelings.

1) _____

_____

_____

_____

2) _____

_____

_____

_____

3) _____

_____

_____

_____

4) _____

_____

_____

_____

5) _____

_____

_____

_____

6) _____

_____

_____

_____

7) _____

_____

_____

_____

If you have thought of your own character conclusions, describe a couple of your best ideas.

1) _____

_____

_____

_____

_____

2) _____
_____
_____
_____
_____
_____

Character Continuations

"That person is a success who has lived well, laughed often, and loved much. They have gained the respect of intelligent humans and the love of children. They have filled their niche and accomplished their task. They leave the world better than they found it. They looked for the best in others and they gave the best they had to give."
~ Harry Emerson Fosdick & Robert Lewis Stevenson

"Take your life in your hands and what happens? A terrible thing: no one to blame."
~ Erica Jong

"You need only claim the events of your life to make yourself yours. When you truly possess all you have been and done, which may take some time, you are fierce with reality. ~ Flonda Scott Maxwell

"Live according to one's Self, not someone else. It's the only way for integrity of one's nature to be preserved." ~ Author Unknown

"Always be a first-rate version of yourself instead of a second-rate version of somebody else." ~ Judy Garland

"Unless you are "THE LATE" you, then it is never too late for you to accomplish your goals, achieve success, and live the life of your dreams!" ~ Andrew S. Taylor

Think your morning JUICE. These six quotes parallel a few concepts from the book's Character Continuations section. For today's journal entry, read each character continuation and describe your inspired thoughts and feelings.

Date: ____/____/____

Read each character continuation and describe your inspired thoughts and feelings.

1) _____

_____

_____

_____

_____

_____

_____

2) _____

_____

_____

_____

_____

_____

_____

3) _____

_____

_____

_____

_____

_____

_____

4) _____

_____

_____

_____

_____

_____

_____

5) _____

_____

_____

_____

_____

_____

6) _____

_____

_____

_____

_____

_____

Create a few of your own character continuations. Describe your best ideas.

1) _____

_____

_____

_____

_____

2) _____

_____

_____

_____

_____

3) _____

_____

_____

_____

_____

_____

4) _____

_____

_____

_____

_____

"No one can make you feel inferior without your consent." ~ Eleanor Roosevelt

"I will not let anyone walk through my mind with dirty feet." ~ Mahatma Gandhi

Think your morning JUICE. These quotes are amazing affirmations. They are also character continuations of Chapter 3's Life Lesson 2: Pain vs. Suffering. The paradigm is feelings are inevitable, but the continuation of feelings is only sustainable if you give your conscious or sub-conscious "consent." So remember the choice is yours. For today's journal entry, read the life-affirming quotes and describe your inspired thoughts and feelings.

Date: _____/_____/_____

Read the life-affirming quotes and describe your inspired thoughts and feelings.

Quote 1) _____

_____

Quote 2) _____

_____

These two quotes inspired me to add a section solely in the workbook...

Biopics/Documentaries— Movies/TV Series

See Category List. Pick one. View it. Describe your inspired thoughts and feelings. Repeat. (Make sure all material is viewed with age appropriateness and audience maturity in mind.)

Historical People: *Braveheart* (William Wallace), *Gandhi*, *JFK*, *The King's Speech* (George VI), *Lawrence of Arabia*, *Lincoln*, *On the Basis of Sex* (Ruth Bader Ginsburg), *Oppenheimer*, *The Queen* (Elizabeth), *The Roosevelts* (Ken Burns Documentary), *Southside with You* (Barack & Michelle Obama), *Spartacus*, *The Butler* (Cecil Gaines), *Wilson*.

Title: _____

_____

_____

_____

_____

_____

_____

_____

_____

_____

_____

_____

_____

_____

_____

_____

_____

_____

People-Who-Saved-Populations-of-People: *Apollo 13, Argo, Erin Brockovich, Hotel Rwanda, Madame Curie, Nicky's Family, 9/11 (2002), Schindler's List, The 33, The Life of Emile Zola, The Story of Louis Pasteur, Sully, Thirteen Lives, World Trade Center.*

Title: _____

_____

_____

_____

_____

_____

_____

_____

_____

_____

_____

_____

_____

_____

_____

_____

_____

_____

_____

_____

_____

_____

_____

_____

_____

Musical People: *8 Mile, Amadeus, The Benny Goodman Story, Bohemian Rhapsody, Coal Miner's Daughter, The Doors, Elvis, Get on Up, The Glenn Miller Story, The Greatest Showman, The Hip Hop Project, Jazz* (Ken Burns Documentary), *La Bamba, Lady Sings the Blues, Maestro, Marley, Nowhere Boy, Notorious, Purple Rain, Ray, Respect, Rocketman, Selena, The Sound of Music, Straight Outta Compton, Sweet Dreams, Taylor Swift: Miss Americana, Walk the Line, Weird: The Al Yankovic Story, What's Love Got to Do with It, Yankee Doodle Dandy.*

Title: _____

_____

_____

_____

_____

_____

_____

_____

_____

_____

_____

_____

_____

_____

_____

_____

_____

_____

_____

_____

_____

Sports People: *42, Air, Ali, Amelia, The Alpinist, Battle of the Sexes, Big George Foreman, The Boys in the Boat, Cinderella Man, The Fighter, Ford v Ferrari, Free Solo* (see Ken Burns' Documentary *The National Parks: America's Best Idea* for more on where this movie was filmed), *Gretzky: The Great One, The Hurricane, Invictus, Invincible, The Jackie Robinson Story, Jim Thorpe – All-American, The Last Dance, Michael Jordan: Air Time, Michael Jordan: Come Fly with Me, Michael Phelps: Medals, Memories & More, Miracle, Moneyball, The Other Shore, Pelé: Birth of a Legend, Prefontaine, The Pride of the Yankees, Race, Remember the Titans, Rudy, Rush, Searching for Bobby Fischer, Somebody Up There Likes Me, Soul Surfer, Space Jam, 30 for 30* (ESPN Films), *True Spirit.*

Title: _____

_____

_____

_____

_____

_____

_____

_____

_____

_____

_____

_____

_____

_____

_____

_____

_____

_____

_____

_____

Newspaper & Radio People: *All the President's Men, Citizen Kane, Good Night, and Good Luck, The Post, The Report, She Said, Spotlight, Stanley and Livingstone, Talk to Me.*

Title: _____

_____

_____

_____

_____

_____

_____

_____

_____

_____

_____

_____

_____

_____

_____

_____

_____

_____

_____

_____

_____

_____

_____

_____

_____

_____

_____

_____

Artist/TV Show/Movie Makers/Book Writer People: *A Beautiful Day in the Neighborhood, Capote, Chaplin, The Fabelmans, Frida, Lust for Life* (Van Gogh), *The Monuments Men, My Left Foot, Pollock, Tolkien, Won't You Be My Neighbor?*

Title: _____

_____

_____

_____

_____

_____

_____

_____

_____

_____

_____

_____

_____

_____

_____

_____

_____

_____

_____

_____

_____

_____

Racial Realities, Sexuality Situations, Real Relationships, Inspiring Innovators People: *12 Years a Slave, BlacKkKlansman, Boys Don't Cry, The Danish Girl, Dallas Buyers Club, Edison, the Man, Flash of Genius, Green Book, Harriet, Hidden Figures, Loving, Malcolm X, Milk, Mississippi Burning, Rustin, Selma, The Social Network, Steve Jobs, The Story of Alexander Graham Bell, Tesla, The Theory of Everything, Tucker: The Man and His Dream.*

Title: _____

_____

_____

_____

_____

_____

_____

_____

_____

_____

_____

_____

_____

_____

_____

_____

_____

_____

_____

_____

_____

_____

_____

War: *12 Strong*, *The American Revolution* (Documentary), *American Sniper*, *Band of Brothers*, *The Civil War* (Ken Burns Documentary), *Glory*, *Hacksaw Ridge*, *The Imitation Game*, *Lone Survivor*, *Midway*, *Napoléon*, *The Pacific*, *Patton*, *Red Tails*, *Thirty Seconds Over Tokyo*, *To Hell and Back*, *The Tuskegee Airmen*, *The U.S. and the Holocaust* (Ken Burns Documentary), *The Vietnam War* (Ken Burns Documentary), *The War* (Ken Burns Documentary), *Windtalkers*.

Title: _____

_____

_____

_____

_____

_____

_____

_____

_____

_____

_____

_____

_____

_____

_____

_____

_____

_____

_____

_____

_____

_____

_____

Your Interests-Hobbies-&-Alternative-Ambition-Peoples: Make a category list of Biopics/Documentaries not already mentioned, the stars/producers/cast/crew etc., are all people with whom you absolutely admire, and the subject material of the movie/TV Series is something you have a high, far above average, abnormal amount of ambition studying!

Title: _____

_____

_____

_____

_____

_____

_____

_____

_____

_____

_____

_____

_____

_____

_____

_____

_____

_____

_____

_____

_____

_____

_____

_____

Non-Non-Fiction People: Make a category list of movies *you would like to be the real-life, in that world, main character!* Review them all. Describe your thoughts and feelings for each. Make sure you show how and why you relate to each character choice from the start of their character arc, where they arrive after the end of the movie journey's end, and where *you* would go and move forward in your character's continuation as you live their lives!

Title: _____

_____

_____

_____

_____

_____

_____

_____

_____

_____

_____

_____

_____

_____

_____

_____

_____

_____

_____

_____

_____

_____

Get GIGSS

"Feedback is the real breakfast of champions." ~ Ken Blanchard and Spencer Johnson

"Keep away from people who try to belittle your ambitions. Small people always do that, but the really great people make you feel, you too can be great." ~ Mark Twain

Think your morning JUICE. Do the following three tasks: First, find as many of these "really great people" as possible. Second, as it is defined in the book, Get GIGSS. And third, have them all over for "the real breakfast of champions." For today's journal entry describe your first impressions of the quotes, my advice, and the book section.

Date: ____/____/____

Describe your first impressions of the quotes, my advice, and the book section.

Quote 1) _____

_____

Quote 2) _____

_____

My advice) _____

_____

The book section) _____

_____

We can't all be spotlight heroes. Someone has to heroically sit in the audience and clap."
~ Will Rogers

"To have great poets, there must be great audiences." ~ Walt Whitman

Think your morning JUICE. These two quotes continue to deal with the concept of everyone has a part to play and even if you are not performing in the center stage spotlight, it doesn't mean you can't be a lead-er. For today's journal entry, read the quotes, consider the concept, and describe your inspired thoughts and feelings.

Date: ____/____/____

Read the quotes, consider the concept, and describe your inspired thoughts and feelings.

Quote 1) _____

_____

Quote 2) _____

_____

The concept) _____

_____

_____

_____

"The human brain can be compared to an electric battery ... a group will provide more energy than one by itself." ~ Napoleon Hill

Think your morning JUICE. I think Napoleon Hill's comparison is perfect. (The definition of a battery starts with, "A number of connected electric cells ..." This sounds like part of the definition of a human brain.) So I hope the quote encourages you to get GIGSS And I also hope these groups of figurative brain batteries completely empowers you to be 100% more productive in your life. For today's journal entry, describe your best, collaborative experience. Answer the questions, "How and why did the participants get together?" "What did you all accomplish?" and "How was the experience beneficial to your life?"

Date: ____/____/____

Describe your best, collaborative experience.

_____

_____

How and why did the participants get together?

_____

_____

What did you all accomplish?

_____

_____

How was the experience beneficial to your life?

_____

_____

Character Clique Switch Day - Exercise 17:

Think your morning JUICE. Use this page to continue or redo Exercise 17. Then, when you have completed the exercise describe your inspired thoughts and feelings.

Date: ____/____/____

_____

_____

_____

_____

_____

_____

_____

_____

_____

_____

_____

_____

_____

_____

_____

_____

_____

_____

_____

_____

_____

_____

_____

_____

_____

_____

_____

_____

_____

_____

_____

_____

_____

_____

_____

_____

_____

_____

_____

_____

_____

_____

_____

CHARACTER CLIQUE SWITCH WEEK				
Monday	Tuesday	Wednesday	Thursday	Friday
Mind-Your-Match-Monday	Tell-It-All-Tuesday	Welcome-To-My-World-Wednesday	Thankful-Thursday	Freaky-Friday

Celebrate Family and Friends!

Andrewism: My Home

I Know, I Have, "The Place" From Where I've Come.

It's, "The Place" From Where I've Been.

I've Left It In The Secure Hands Of, "Mother Nature" And, "Father Time."

These, "Guardians," Are, "Forever" And, "Timeless."

I've Made A Promise: "I'm Going To Go Back There Someday."

The Fulfillment Of This Promise Is Both Possible And Impossible.

I Know, Life Is A One-Way Trip.

The Present Is A Gift. … Always Arriving.

Life Is Entirely Encapsulated In Every New, Magical, Moment.

The Present Is Reality As Seen By The Beholder.

I Know, I Can Physically Find,

All The Human-Made Roads,

My Past's Address,

The Technical, Tangible, Geographic Location, Of What Was Once, "My House."

I Will, Say To Myself, "This Used To Be, "My Playground.""

Become Simply, "A Guest."

Climb The, "Now-Seems-Quite-Small-Staircase."

Enter What Was Once, "My Room."

Remember With, "My Mind."

Reclaim What Was, "Never Really Given Away."

Follow The Path Of, "My Memory."

Imagine The Images Of, "My Yesteryears."

I Will, See The Panoramic Picture.

Look All Around The House.

See Where All Our Outdoor Objects Once Stood.

Look All Throughout The House.

See A Kaleidoscopic View.

Look And See Both Reality And Remembrance.

I Will, Superimpose Everything, With A Multitude Of Multi-Colored, Childhood Images.

Unveil The Secrets That Are Hidden By The Ebbs & Flows Of Nature & Time.

Visualize, "The Place," Again.

Realize I Physically Did Not Have To Travel The Trip.

Understand, "The Place," Has Always Been Inside, "My Mind."

Feel It Is A Special, Irreplaceable Part Of, "Who I Am Now!"

Recognize, "Myself," "My Family," And, "My Friends."

Equate Them, With, "The Place." "The Place" Is, "Where I Hang My Heart."

I Will, Know, "The Place," Is, "My Home."

Think your morning JUICE. I put this *Andrewism* poetry piece, here for two reasons. First, it was inspired by my family and friends. And second, it also supports the concept of how home is where you hang your heart. For today's journal entry, read the *Andrewism* poetry piece, consider the concept, and describe your inspired thoughts and feelings. Then, if you want, write your own, family and friends, "My Home," inspired poetry piece.

Date: ____/____/____

Read the *Andrewism* poetry piece, consider the concept, and describe your inspired thoughts and feelings.

_____

_____

_____

_____

_____

_____

If you want, write your own family and friends, "My Home" inspired poetry piece.

Title:_____

_____

_____

_____

_____

_____

_____

_____

_____

_____

_____

_____

_____

_____

Andrewism: An Angel: Also Known As... & Anyone's Answer Is Acceptable

In The Eye Of This Beholder,
I Believe There Are Angels Among Us.
(In My Holistic Heart And My Metaphysical Mind:)
My Questions, Inspired By This Thought, Are As Follows: ... What Are Angels? (&) Who Are Angels? ... What Are Angels? ...   ... Angels Are ... Also Known As ... Someone Who Is ...
... A "Family-Friend."
... A "Stand By Me" And "Lean On Me" Model For The Music.
... A "Daily Doer Of Random Acts Of Kindness."
... A "Snuggler" And A Masterful "Maker Of Lover."
... A "Gershinesque" Watcher Over You.   (And)
... A "Pleasant Provider" Of A Wonderfully Welcome, Warm, Unsolicited, Gentle Touch On Your Shoulder. (This Touch Always Brings You Back "Home" When You're Lost, Deep In Thought.)
                    ... Angels Are ... Also Known As ...
... Someone's Whose "Spirit Cup" Runneth Over Into Yours & Subsequently Sweetened Your Life.
... Someone Who, Thinks The Thought And Communicates The Compliment.   (And)
... Someone Who, Does The Duteous Acts Of Heroism, No One Ever Sees, Except For The Actors And The Actees. Ok. You Get The Idea. These Are My Ideas.
          Who Are Angels? ...   ... Angels Are ... Anyone's Answer Is Acceptable. ...
... The Point Is, We All Have Our Own Images, Role Models, Definitions, & Definers Of The Term.
... The Point Is, We All Know One When We See One.
... And For Those Who Know One Personally, Tell Them Today! Do The Deed! Say The Words!
... With Your Magical Message, Create For Them "Heaven On Earth!"
... Don't Let The Moment Get Any Older!
... Say, "Hear Me! Here & Now! YOU ARE AN ANGEL! ... In The Eyes Of This Beholder!"

Think your morning JUICE. Recently, *It's A Wonderful Life* was voted Number One Most Inspiring Movie Of All Time.* (*See AFI's *100 Years 100 Cheers*.) In it, George Bailey learns how, "One life touches so many other lives." And, "No one is a failure who has friends." George's teacher is Clarence Oddbody, ASII (Angel, 2nd Class.) In the last scene a bell rings and we know Clarence has earned his wings. For today's journal entry, read the *Andrewism* poetry piece and describe your inspired thoughts and feelings. Then, write about a few of your life's most valuable, absolute angels. Describe how they earned their wings and explain how they continue to be beneficial.* (*Putting this in writing and sharing it, is a wonderful way to acknowledge and celebrate family and friends.) Finally, if you want, write your own angel inspired poetry piece.

Date: ____/____/____

Read the *Andrewism* poetry piece, and describe your inspired thoughts and feelings.

_____

_____

_____

_____

Write about a few of your life's most valuable, absolute angels (AA).

1) _____

_____

_____

_____

_____

_____

2) _____

_____

_____

_____

_____

_____

3) _____

_____

_____

_____

_____

_____

4) _____

_____

_____

_____

_____

_____

If you want, write your own, angel inspired poetry piece.

Title:_____

_____

_____

_____

_____

_____

_____

_____

_____

_____

_____

_____

"A true friend is nature's masterpiece." ~ Ralph Waldo Emerson

"A friend is a gift you give to yourself." ~ Robert Louis Stevenson

"Life is fortified by friendships. To love and be loved is the greatest happiness." ~ Sydney Smith

"The best service a friend can do is help you keep your courage by holding a mirror in which you can see a noble image of yourself." ~ George Bernard Shaw

Think your morning JUICE. These four quotes are about what it means to be a true friend. For today's journal entry, read each quote and describe your inspired thoughts and feelings. Then, write your own definition. (Fill in the blank. A true friend is …) Finally, describe someone special who truly matches your definition.

Date: ____/____/____

Read each quote and describe your inspired thoughts and feelings.

Quote 1) _____

_____

_____

_____

Quote 2) _____

_____

_____

_____

Quote 3) _____

_____

_____

_____

Quote 4) _____

_____

_____

_____

Fill in the blank. A true friend is _____

_____

_____

_____

Describe someone special who truly matches your definition.

_____

_____

_____

_____

Create Unity and Community!

"No one is an island. Everyone is simply a single part of the main body." ~ John Donne

"No matter what world we live in now, we are all people of The Earth, connected to one another by our mutual, and equal, humanity." ~ Angeles Arrien

"The Earth provides enough to satisfy everyone's needs, but not everyone's greed."
~ Mahatma Gandhi

"May all beings everywhere be awakened, healed, peaceful, and free: May there be peace in the world, and an end to war, poverty, violence, and oppression; and may we all (arrive in this new world) together." ~ Lama Surya Das

"An individual has not started living, until (they) can rise above, the narrow confines of individualistic concerns, to the higher, broader concerns of all humanity."
~ Martin Luther King Jr.

"We begin from the premise, all beings cherish happiness and do not want suffering. It then becomes both morally wrong and pragmatically unwise to pursue only your own happiness (and to be) oblivious to the feelings and aspirations of all others who surround us as members of the same human family. The wiser course, is to (also) think of others, whenever (we are) pursuing our own happiness." ~ The 14th Dalai Lama

Think your morning JUICE. These six quotes share the common theme of encouraging the reader to create unity and community. For today's journal entry, read each quote and describe your inspired thoughts and feelings. Then, write your own definition. (Fill in the blank. A world which creates unity and community is …)

Date: ____/____/____

Read each quote and describe your inspired thoughts and feelings.

Quote 1) _____

_____

_____

_____

Quote 2) _____

_____

Quote 3) _____

_____

_____

_____

Quote 4) _____

_____

_____

_____

Quote 5) _____

_____

_____

_____

Quote 6) _____

_____

_____

_____

Fill in the blank. A world which creates unity and community is ...

_____

_____

_____

_____

Post View

"Determining to follow your dreams, passionately express yourself, and live life to the fullest; this is the greatest gift you can give to those you love, and to yourself."
~ Laurence G. Boldt

Think your morning JUICE. For today's journal entry, do the following three reviews. First, review your five finished activities. 1) A Character Commitment Contract, 2) A My Mission Statement & My Purpose In Life Paragraph, 3) A My Definition Of Success Essay, 4) A My Funeral & Epitaph Plan, (and hopefully you have done) 5) A Character Clique Switch Day. (And hopefully you have already compiled and organized your final results.) Second, review today's quote. And third, review a few favorite concepts from Chapter 6. After each review describe your present day, inspired thoughts and feelings. And when you are finally finished, start your journey in Chapter 7: Behind The Scenes!

Date: ____/____/____

Review your five finished activities and describe your present day, inspired thoughts and feelings.

Character Commitment Contract

_____

_____

_____

_____

_____

_____

My Mission Statement & My Purpose In Life Paragraph

_____

_____

_____

_____

_____

_____

My Definition Of Success Essay

_____
_____
_____
_____
_____
_____

My Funeral & Epitaph Plan

_____
_____
_____
_____
_____
_____

Character Clique Switch Day

_____
_____
_____
_____
_____
_____

Review the quote and describe your present day, inspired thoughts and feelings.

_____
_____
_____
_____

Review a few favorite concepts from Chapter 6 and describe your present day, inspired thoughts and feelings.

1) _____

_____

_____

_____

2) _____

_____

_____

_____

3) _____

_____

_____

_____

4) _____

_____

_____

_____

Extra Expressings and Thoughtful Thinkings: Positivity Paragraphs

How You Do Every Little Thing Is How You Do
EVERY-BIG-THING! … Make sure this is true …
When you know it's true: No-One watching you!
When you know it means not as much to you!
When you know it matters the most to you!
When you know it's life's consistency for you!
When you know it's Code-Of-Conduct for you!
When you know There's-No-Other-Way-To-LIVE!
FOR-YOU-TO-BE-TRUE-FOR-YOU-DOING-YOU!

Write your inspired thoughts and feelings.
_____
_____
_____
_____
_____
_____
_____
_____

WORDS: Wonderments With Multiple Meanings!
Not often I'm ever at a longtime loss for words!
For GREAT-FULL-LY, GENUINLY, & TRULY, …
I ALWAYS KNOW: Thank You! See You! & YES!
[Ultimately & Unconditionally] … I LOVE YOU!
These words have so many multiple aptitudes!
Co-Workers, Coaches, Team-Mates, Teachers!
Students, Real-Role-Models, Lifetime-Leaders!
Friends, Family, & ULTIMATELY YOURSELF!

Write your inspired thoughts and feelings.
_____
_____
_____
_____
_____
_____
_____
_____

MY CONCLUSIONS & MY CONTINUATIONS:
MY 56th Year: Living an Aliving-A-Lot Lifetime!
MY 12+Books: All are my Beyond-ME-Babies!
MY Website: TaylorEDTime Tech-Immortality!
MY Positivity Paragraphs: Gifts & Presents!
MY Joyous Journaling: Life's Joy-Full Journey!
MY Family & Friends: They are my Foundation!
MY Life-Time Teachings: MY LOVE & LEGACY!
MY Forecast: MY FULLY FANTASTIC FUTURE!

Write your inspired thoughts and feelings.
_____
_____
_____
_____
_____
_____
_____
_____

LIFE: It's The SHORTEST & The LONGEST!
It's made up of a multitude of milliseconds!
It's the longest experience you'll ever live!
It's The COMMONEST & The UNIQUEST!
It's Bestowed On All & You're An Only You!
So I Soul-Fully Say To You A Total Truth!
LIFE: It's Yours! & MAKE IT FANTASTIC!
& For Harmony & Happiness To Find You …
DO 42!A.K.A. Whatever Works For You! !

Write your inspired thoughts and feelings.
_____
_____
_____
_____
_____
_____
_____
_____

Family & Friends: Give the gift of your present!
Call any cool characters from your clan!
Talk with any teammates from your tribe!
Contact any colleagues from your contacts!
E-Mail any of your energizers & empowerers!
Text any of your lifetime, totally topers!
Message any of your love-a-lot, magic makers!
DO THIS EVERYDAY! In some simple way!
This way, you'll feel LOVE, FOR-EVER-Y-DAY!

CLOSE YOUR EYES! MAKE A WISH! BELIEVE!
KNOW! In A Wonderful-Way, It Will Come TRUE!
IF You Are ALL COMMMITED TO YOUR CAUSE!
IF You Are FIRMLY FOCUSED IN YOUR VISION!
IF You Are PERSISTENT TO YOUR PURPOSE!
IF You Are WHOLLY WILLING TO WORK HARD!
IF You Are OPEN TO SPECIAL SERENDIPITIES
IF You Are ABLE TO NEVER GIVE UP! EVER! &
IF You Are SPECIFIC TO SEE YOUR SUCCESS!

Write your inspired thoughts and feelings.

_____
_____
_____
_____
_____
_____
_____
_____

Write your inspired thoughts and feelings.

_____
_____
_____
_____
_____
_____
_____
_____

Okay. Now turn the page.

CHAPTER 7:
BEHIND THE SCENES AND EPILOGUE!

The Final Fanfare: Tap Into Your SOUL (Spirit Of Ultimate LOVE (Living Only Vibrant Energies))! & Live The Life FANTASTIC!

Andrewism: Life: As Seen By The Sky's Eyes &
Life: As Sown In The Tapestry Of Time!

I Have Taken, "The Path Less Traveled By," And For I, "It Has Made All The Difference."
Oh Yes! Oh My!
Here Am I, On My, Present Point Time Line, And My Linear Life Thread.
It Is A Life Line, Which Began Way Back In My Baby Bed!

I Sigh, And I Ask Why, Am I Here?
Have I, Really Made A Difference Down Here?
Good Questions! Oh Dear!
I Ask The Sky's Eyes, For They Can See Me Quite Clear!

They Reply, And They Say, "Today You Can Not See, All Of You, -- AKA -- A Holistic Me!
Your Soul's Goal Should Be, To Just Be, Patient, Have Faith, And Keep A Steady Pace.
Life Is A Journey, In A Tapestry Of Time.
Only With The Sky's Eyes, Can You Truly See The Grand Design!

Look Back To The Path. The Past Is Old Lessons Learned. It Should Be Left Far Behind.
If You Try To Live There, You'll Get Burned, "Nothing New," Is All You, Will Ever Find!
As For The Future, It Is Equal In Kind.
You See, You Cannot See, Foresight Is Truly Blind.

So My Friend, Do Not Dwell On How Life Will End, Or
What Waits Around The River's Bend, Or
What Life There Is Still Left To See,
On The Sunny Side Of That There Tree.

Just Live Life Fully,
In The Gift That Is Your Present.
For Truly, It Is The Only,
"Perfect Place," For You To Holistically Be!"

Think your morning JUICE. Here's The Final Fanfare: Tap Into Your SOUL! And Live The Life FANTASTIC! This is where our journey ends and your journey begins. In short, IT'S PARTY TIME! I've saved this *Andrewism* poetry piece for this final chapter because it encourages you to do an "overview" of your life. For today's journal entry, read the *Andrewism* poetry piece, and describe your inspired thoughts and feelings.

Date: _____/_____/_____

Read the *Andrewism* poetry piece, and describe your inspired thoughts and feelings.

_____

_____

_____

_____

_____

_____

"(Everyone's) role, is to fulfill his or her purpose through a sincere heart, which is in harmony with all creation and has a love of all things." ~ Morihei Ueshiba

Think your morning JUICE. I have read several books on the philosophy of Aikido. (See *The Way Of Aikido: Life Lessons From An American Sensai* By George Leonard.) With the possible exception of Tai Chi, I believe the philosophy of Aikido promotes the highest degree of how you should live your life in harmony with your surroundings. For today's journal entry, read the quote and do your own research and reading on the philosophy of Aikido. Then, describe your inspired thoughts and feelings.

Date: _____/_____/_____

Read the quote and do your own research and reading on the philosophy of Aikido. Then, describe your inspired thoughts and feelings.

_____

_____

_____

_____

_____

_____

"All the arts we practice are apprenticeships. The greatest art is the masterpiece of your life." ~ M. C. Richards

"A Perfect You is your masterpiece! Be proud! Show it to the world!"~ Andrew S. Taylor

Think your morning JUICE. After completing six chapters of character creation and construction I hope these two quotes encourage you to evaluate yourself as a true work of art and a real life, "masterpiece." For today's journal entry, read the two quotes and describe your inspired thoughts and feelings.

Date: ____/____/____

Read the two quotes and describe your inspired thoughts and feelings.

Quote 1) _____

_____

_____

_____

Quote 2) _____

_____

_____

_____

"I would much rather seriously struggle, and succeed in altruism, than play-it-safe, and wallow in apathy." ~ Andrew S. Taylor

Think your morning JUICE. It was tough to know where to put this quote. First, I thought it should be at the beginning to give encouragement as you start on the path toward self-improvement. Next, I thought it should be at the end so you'd feel a strong sense of satisfaction knowing I'm now positively preaching to the choir. Then, I realized placing it here serves both schools of thought because Chapter 7 is both the end of our journey and the beginning of yours. For today's journal entry read the quote, see how far you have come on our journey, and know you are now really ready to set sail on your journey. Then describe your inspired thoughts and feelings.

Date: ____/____/____

Read the quote, consider the writing prompts. Describe your inspired thoughts and feelings.

_____

_____

_____

_____

_____

_____

"Determine to play your part in creating the world you want to live in." ~ Laurence G. Boldt

"What we do is only a (single) drop in the ocean, but if we didn't do it, the ocean would be one drop less." ~ Mother Teresa

"Like the proverbial pebble dropped into a still pond, the shifts of consciousness we make in our (present day,) personal lives, send out small, but important, waves, which ripple through the whole world (and throughout all future time.)" ~ Shakti Gawain

"A human is a part of the whole we call the universe, a single part limited in time and space. They experience themselves, their thoughts and feelings, as something separated from the rest - a kind of optical illusion of their own consciousness. This illusion is a prison for us, restricting us to our own personal desires, and to sharing affection for only the select few people who are closest to us. Our life task must be to embrace all living beings and all of nature, which is in the whole universe." ~ Albert Einstein

Think your morning JUICE. In short, you are a part of the whole, not apart from the whole. So promise yourself you will be the lead-er and you will play the part of your life. For today's journal entry, read each quote and describe your inspired thoughts and feelings.

Date: ____/____/____

Read each quote and describe your inspired thoughts and feelings.

Quote 1) _____

_____

_____

_____

Quote 2) _____

_____

_____

_____

Quote 3) _____

_____

_____

_____

Quote 4) _____

_____

_____

_____

"Our greatest power is the power of choice. We decide where we are, what we think, and what we do. No one can take this power away without our permission." ~ Author Unknown

Think your morning JUICE. This quote is an absolutely right reminder. With each piece of advice in this book, you have the final choice. Take it or leave it. It is your life. For today's journal entry, revisit your favorite chapter sections. Describe how choosing to follow the section's advice, has ultimately improved your life.

Date: ____/____/____

Pick your favorite chapter sections. Write an Advice Summary Statement. Describe how your life has improved.

Chapter 1) Section Title: _____

Advice Summary Statement: _____

_____

Life Improvement: _____

_____

_____

_____

Chapter 2) Section Title: _____

Advice Summary Statement: _____

_____

Life Improvement: _____

_____

_____

_____

Chapter 3) Section Title: _____

Advice Summary Statement: _____

_____

Life Improvement: _____

_____

_____

_____

Chapter 4) Section Title: _____

Advice Summary Statement: _____

_____

Life Improvement: _____

_____

_____

Chapter 5) Section Title: _____

Advice Summary Statement: _____

_____

Life Improvement: _____

_____

_____

_____

Chapter 6) Section Title: _____

Advice Summary Statement: _____

_____

Life Improvement: _____

_____

_____

_____

"The world of reality has its limits; the world of imagination is boundless." ~ Rousseau

"There is no, life I know, quite like pure imagination." ~ Gene Wilder as Willy Wonka

"Imagination is more important than knowledge." ~ Albert Einstein

"Without the activity of playing with fantasy, no creative work has ever yet come to birth. The debt we owe to the play of the imagination is incalculable." ~ C. G. Jung

Think your morning JUICE. These quotes have a common theme. They show the importance of imagination. So as you journey beyond this book and continue to construct your new and improved self-helped character, insist on imagining new horizons. Dare to dream big and you'll find the most wonderful of all worlds: Your Highest, Best Self! For today's journal entry, read each quote and describe your inspired thoughts and feelings. Then, describe a couple delightfully dreamed and ingeniously imagined new horizons.

Date: _____/_____/_____

Read each quote and describe your inspired thoughts and feelings.

Quote 1) _____

_____

_____

_____

Quote 2) _____

_____

_____

_____

Quote 3) _____

_____

_____

_____

Quote 4) _____

_____

_____

_____

Describe a couple delightfully dreamed and ingeniously imagined new horizons.

1) _____

_____

_____

_____

2) _____

_____

_____

_____

Andrewism: A Sound Life!

What We Call A, "Tree," Falls In,
What We Call A, "Forest." Is There,
What We Call A, "Sound?"
Note: No One Noticed. No One Heard. ... This Is,
    What We Call An, "Of Course!" Yes! There Is A, "Sound."
What We Call A, "Human Doing," Lives In,
What We Call A, "World." Is That,
What We Call A, "Sound Life?"
Note: The, "Public Eye," Did Not Notice. The, "Public Ear," Did Not Hear. ... This Is,
    What We Call An, "Of Course!" Yes! This Is A, "Sound Life."
What We Call, "Fame," It Be Not, Every Soul's Goal. But Truly,
What We Call A, "Life," With A, "Name," Weather It Be, "Great," Or, "Small," It Is,
What We Call A, "Priceless Possession." It Is What We Call, "Very Valuable,"
For One, And For All!

Think your morning JUICE. This *Andrewism* poetry piece, was inspired by the old, philosophical, brainteaser, riddle question, "If a tree falls in the forest and nobody is there to hear the event, does the tree technically make a sound?" (If you Google search, "If a tree falls" you will learn more about this question and its multiple possible answers.) For today's journal entry, read the *Andrewism* poetry piece, and describe your inspired thoughts and feelings. Then, if you want, consider the poem's message, and write your own poetry piece.

Date: ____/____/____

Read the *Andrewism* poetry piece, and describe your inspired thoughts and feelings.

_____

_____

_____

_____

_____

_____

_____

_____

_____

_____

If you want, consider the poem's message, and write your own poetry piece.

Title:_____

_____

_____

_____

_____

_____

_____

_____

_____

_____

_____

_____

_____

_____

_____

_____

_____

_____

_____

_____

_____

_____

Look at the photo above. Write your thoughts and feelings.

_____

_____

_____

_____

_____

_____

_____

_____

_____

_____

_____

_____

_____

_____

_____

_____

Look at the photo above. Write your thoughts and feelings.

_____

_____

_____

_____

_____

_____

_____

_____

_____

_____

_____

_____

_____

_____

Sunset *AND* Sunrise!!

May your life be a joy-full journey doing dramatic destinations and living LOVE-fully in absolutely amazing, ALIVING abundance!!

"It's not the mountain summit we conquer but ourselves." ~ Edmund Hillary

"The real Tragedy is the tragedy of the man who never in his life braces himself for his one supreme effort-he never stretches to his full capacity, never stands up to his full stature." ~ Arnold Bennett

"Far better it is to dare mighty things, to win glorious triumphs even though checkered by failure, than to rank with those poor spirits, who neither enjoy, nor suffer much, because they live in a gray twilight, that knows neither victory nor defeat." ~ Theodore Roosevelt

"To be what we are, and to do what we are capable of doing, this is the only way to (live) your life." ~ Robert Louis Stevenson

"The soul grows well when it is giving and receiving love. Love, after all, is a verb, an action word, not a noun." ~ Joan Borysenko

"Creative powers grow and develop through use; the more you challenge yourself, the more you will grow." ~ Laurence G. Boldt

"Every exit is an entry to somewhere else." ~ Tom Stoppard

"We are all wanderers on this earth. Our hearts are full of wonder and our souls are deep with dreams." ~ Traveler Proverb

"It is good to have an end to journey toward; but truly it's the journey that matters in the end." ~ Ursula K. Le Guin

"The path of personal growth leads upward, through the gauntlet of human experience to the peaks of our potential." ~ Dan Millman

"No matter where you go there you are." ~ Peter Weller as Buckaroo Banzi

"The human race has only one chance for survival and true advancement. Our capacity for negativization must be matched and subsequently surpassed, by our capacity for positivization." ~ Andrew S. Taylor

Think your morning JUICE. These twelve quotes are my final fanfare, words of wisdom. I use the Buckaroo Banzi quote to remind me how far I've traveled on my journey. I used this same quote in my 1987 high school yearbook. I also said, "Graduation! I like this plan!

I am glad to be a part of it!" But anyway, back to the task at hand. For today's journal entry, read each quote and describe your inspired thoughts and feelings.

Date: ____/____/____

Read each quote and describe your inspired thoughts and feelings.

Quote 1) _____

_____

_____

_____

Quote 2) _____

_____

_____

_____

Quote 3) _____

_____

_____

_____

Quote 4) _____

_____

_____

_____

Quote 5) _____

_____

_____

_____

Quote 6) _____

_____

Quote 7) _____

_____

_____

_____

Quote 8) _____

_____

_____

_____

Quote 9) _____

_____

_____

_____

Quote 10) _____

_____

_____

_____

Quote 11) _____

_____

_____

_____

Quote 12) _____

_____

_____

_____

"Life is a…
Life is a song… sing it.
Life is a game… play it.
Life is a challenge… meet it.
Life is a dream… realize it.
Life is a sacrifice… offer it.
Life is a love… live it and love it." ~ Sai Baba

Andrewism: … Life … Or … Movie … & … Movie … Or … Life …

It Has A Definitive Beginning, Middle, And End.
It Has Lows And Highs.
It Has A Collected Cast Of Supporting Characters.
It Has Negatives And Positives.
It Has A Vast Variety Of Possible, Potential, Lessons To Be Learned.
It Has Reality And Magic.
It Has A Complex And Complicated Gestation And Creation Process.
It Has Time Limits And Time Transcendence.
It Has A Self-Conducted Sense Of Rhythm.
It Has Frigid Facts And Aesthetic Artistry.
It Has A Permanent Place In Holistic History.
It Has Disorientation And Balance.
It Has A Self-Determined Reason For Being.
It Has Logic And Emotions.
It Has A Condition Where, "It" Is Its Only Priceless Possession.
It Has …
It Is A … *

Think your morning JUICE. This quote and *Andrewism* poetry piece, remind me of a lyric line from The Muppet Movie's song, The Rainbow Connection. It says, "Life's like a movie, write your own ending, keep believing, keep pretending, we've done just what we've set out to do." For today's journal entry, read the quote and *Andrewism* poetry piece, describe your inspired thoughts and feelings, and write your own, Life Is A … , self- inspiring quote. Then, as our journey in the book and workbook cordially comes to a conclusion, "write your own ending, keep believing, keep pretending, (and keep doing) just what (you've) set out to do."

Date: ____/____/____

Read the quote and *Andrewism* poetry piece. Describe your inspired thoughts and feelings.

_____

_____

_____

_____

Write your own Life is a ... , self-inspiring quote.

Title: Life is a _____

_____

_____

_____

_____

_____

_____

_____

_____

_____

_____

_____

When you finish writing your "Life is a..." quote, this small space is yours to doodle with it whatever you want.

"There are two ways to live: you can live as if nothing is a miracle; you can live as if everything is a miracle." ~ Albert Einstein

Andrewism: Today: It's Your Life, Sail Away & Play!

Today, As Always, Is A Day Of Arrivals And Departures.
>You Are Leaving, Your Life, Old.
>You Are Living, Your Life, New.

Today, On Queue, You Are Waiting On A Wind.
>You Want It To Fill Your Sails.
>You Want It To Carry You Away.
>Far Or Near, Anywhere But Here, And My Dear,
>Who Or What, Puts That Wind In Your Sails Is Entirely Up To You

Today, Please Do, Be True, To Yourself, & Remember,
>Don't Leave Any Dream, Up On The Shelf. Pack Everything!
>After All, Experience, Enthusiasm, And Extra Energy,
>Are All Easy, "Carry On Items."
>That You Should Keep With You At All Times.

Today, You View, & You Look Back On Your Landly Path, And You See That,
>For The Past Few Years, You Knew, What You Needed To Do.
>You Are The One, That Got The Job Done, And
>Now, At Last, This Is The Last Day,
>Of The Rest Of Your Life.

Today, Nothing New, Everyone's Question To You,
>What Do You Want To Do,
>With Your Life?

Today, I Give To You, A Recommended Response.
>You Should Say,
>"I Want To Play! Okay?!"   In Conclusion:

Today, I Say To You, As I Sit Here On The Dock Of The Bay, And
>As I Watch The Tide Of You Roll Away,
>In My Viewed Vision, It's Okay, With Me. You See, I Believe You've Earned It Today!

And So, With Love, And Wishes Of Fair Wind, Calm Seas, And Good Speed,
>I Will Send You On Your Way, Down Your Own Personal Stream Of Dreams.
>As I Say To You, (Quote:) (It's Your Life.) "Do Or Do Not, There Is No Try!" (Yoda)
>I Hope You Will Always Be Able To Fly High On My Version Of, "A Good-Bye Wave!"
>"Take What You Got & Fly With It!" (Jim Henson)

Think your morning JUICE. This is the last *Andrewism* poetry piece. As the writing process of this workbook comes to an end, I hope it eloquently conveys my final thoughts and feelings. For today's journal entry, read the *Andrewism* poetry piece and describe your inspired thoughts and feelings.

Date: ____/____/____

Read the *Andrewism* poetry piece, and describe your inspired thoughts and feelings.

_____

_____

_____

_____

_____

_____

_____

_____

_____

_____

_____

_____

"A journey of a thousand miles begins and ends with just one step." ~ Lao Tzu

Think your morning JUICE. This is the last quote to appear in the workbook. It is also no coincidence, it was the first quote I used in Chapter 1. As intended, the process has come full circle. For today's journal entry, read the quote and describe your inspired thoughts and feelings. (1) Then, as you complete *our* journey, of reading and writing in this self-help book and workbook, faithfully begin *your* journey, and write your final fanfare, first flight, overall thoughts and feelings. (2)

Date: ____/____/____

1) _____

_____

_____

_____

_____

_____

_____

_____

2) _____

_____

_____

_____

_____

_____

_____

_____

_____

_____

_____

_____

GOOD LUCK IN ALL OF YOUR LIFE'S CHARACTER CREATIONS!
THANK YOU FOR READING AND DOING EVERYTHING!
YOUR CHARACTER CREATION COACH
AND ENTERTAINING EDUCATOR,

Andrew S. Taylor

P.S.: PERSONAL SENTIMENTALITY!!
ALL MY LIFE: I dreamed dreams and whole-heartedly believed
all of them will come totally true FOR ME!
EVERY EXPERIENCE: I lived physically, intellectually, emotionally, and spiritually
HOLISTICALLY HONEST!
ALL MY FRIENDS: I gave great gratitude for all the quantity of real quality time
graciously given TO ME!
EVERY DAY ALIVE: I learned absolute appreciation for
Self, Occupations, Relationships, Time-Transitions. EVERYTHING!
ALL MY FAMILY: I embraced my most impassioned code of conduct!
I'm a collaboration culmination! IT IS ME!
EVERY & ALL MY LOVE(S): I returned wonderfully worthy of them all!
I AM NOW MY BEST TaylorED Time LIFE!

A+

Blank Page for Additional Notes

Blank Page for Additional Notes

Blank Page for Additional Notes

Blank Page for Additional Notes

ABOUT THE AUTHOR

Andrew S. Taylor holds two BSED degrees in Pre-K-12, Elementary and Secondary Education Theater/Speech. As a self-employed entrepreneur, he is a teenage through adult Life Enrichment Teacher, Creativity Workshop Facilitator, Special Event Public Speaker, and Personal/Professional Life Coach/Consultant. He is equally proficient with individuals, couples, and large-scale groups. At Interlochen National Arts Camp, he was Divisional Honor Camper ('87 H.S.B. Theater Major) and Honor Cabin Counselor ('05 & '07). He was his university's Muppet Mascot, The OU Bobcat, a Pre-K-12 Child Care Teacher/Program Director for eight years, and also The Children's Department Supervisor & Storytime Reader, at a super-sized Barnes & Noble, for four years.

When not every day, enthusiastically engaged in creative writing, his hobbies include collating his colossal collection of Movies & TV Shows (2,800+DISKS!), making beaded jewelry (pins, necklaces, and friendship bracelets), and acting in Community Theater. Mr. Taylor lives in Ann Arbor, MI, and can be contacted at www.TaylorEDTime.com.

BE A PART OF *LIFELINES OF LIFETIMES!*

As soon as I get enough entries, I'll put together a compilation book, entitled *Lifelines of Lifetimes!* Each story entry will be a mini biography of someone who is UN-famous and has created countless personal, invisible MINEs (Moment Immortal Never Ending).

*See the *Andrewism* poetry piece entitled, "I Want My Life MINEs."

If you have someone in mind, you wish to honor in epitaph memory, or as a living, loving, Lifetime Achievement Award, then please submit/attach, your PDF word document/entry, to the following e-mail address, and use this subject line:

Andrew S. Taylor: The Lifelines of Lifetimes Project!

Drewman42@Yahoo.com

Please use American Typewriter - Condensed font, 12-point size, and 1.5 space. Please include a short, bio paragraph, which explains who you are and your connection to the person you are profiling.

ALIVINGLY42!!

ANDREW S. TAYLOR

A+

OTHER BOOKS BY ANDREW S. TAYLOR

TaylorED Time: How to Dramatically Build Your Character & Live the Life FANTASTIC!*
***Full and Novel, Thriving and Successful, Totally In Control**

All right! Action! The world's your stage! It's time to play the part of Your Life! Time to DO A Perfect You!

Don't leave anything to chance! Do it with MAGIC (Make A Good Intelligent Choice)! Do it TODAY! Do it NOW!

This is an engaging and empowering self-help book for teens-adults. Andrew S. Taylor blends his background of theater, teaching, and coaching, to show a step-by-step practical plan: *how to dramatically improve your life!*

Within its poignant pages, you will:
Forge your foundation and follow the simple steps of Character Crystallization!

Take Character and Self-Inventory.	Presentize Yourself!
Find True (For You) North!	Set Sail for your FANTASTIC future!

Define the definitive difference between Human Being vs. Human Doing!

Traverse four stages of your self's-situation.	Reflexively Re-Acting vs. Actively Acting.
Focus and Pay Attention!	And, (when you're given) Help: Earn It!

See the sights so you clearly See the Scene!

Hind, Fore, Now, BEAUTIFUL In: 1 Way Sights.	Holistic Intimacy: The Truest 2 Way Sight.
Explore The Hierarchy of Human Sexuality.	Learn Life Lessons: School is Always in Session!

SORT Your Life so you easily Set the Stage!

Facilitate your Four-File System.	Self, Occupations, Relationships, Time-Transitions.
Differentiate: Lonely vs. Alone.	Set Your (Mind's) Set: It Takes All Kinds to Make a World!

Adjust your attitude and be your own beholder of The Heart of Your Art!

Pinpoint Your Passions!	Eliminate forecasting FEAR! Do What FUELs You!
Be Perceptive from Your Perspective!	Be Persistent to Your Purpose!

Discover the dramatic difference between being Content and Comfortable vs. Happy and Hungry!

Complete your character construction and arrive at The Curtain Call!

Do Character Conclusions and Continuations.	Get GIGSS. Take total responsibility for your life.
Celebrate Family and Friends!	Create Unity and Community!

Determine your definition of success and write-ly make your life's major mission statement.

AND with this wonderful way, you will learn to consciously live the rest of your life by choice, not by chance!

Everything is set! Sit down. Get completely comfortable. Get gloriously geeked. Look and read what's within!

Our journey is about to begin!

Children's Books

BIRDS!

Within these poignant pages, you will read about and review the colorful and complete world of all our feathered friends. See birds from far and near and explore their extensive, worldwide diversities. In the end, you will recognize and learn, despite all their differences, they are all still first and foremost, foundationally, one family of birds! Yes it is true: each individual is special and unique. And so, also thus, in perfect parallel, they are all just like us!

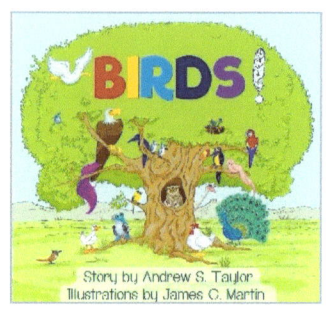

Author Andrew S. Taylor and Illustrator James G. Martin take you on this vibrant and visual display of diversity of all the spectacular spectrum of beautiful birds. And you will ultimately see, how all that in totality, transparently translates into reality, to the whole planetary population of humanity, all around our wonderful world!

The Phenomenal Phoenix!

Within these poignant pages, you will effortlessly explore the expanded dictionary definition and the everlasting legend of The Phenomenal Phoenix! This beautiful bird will teach you much more than merely magical flying. Its spectacular story will show you how to take what you've got and fly with it!

Author Andrew S. Taylor and Illustrator James G. Martin bring this magical bird, and life lesson, ALIVE! Delve deeper between the lines. Go beyond the fictional fiery feathers. Discover how inside all of us there is a soaring spirit of strength that fortifies our very real and always at the ready, regal resilience. And with those character qualities, any and all adversity can be overtly overcome!

Something Small

Within these poignant pages, you will see how the something small, simple little things, do make a miraculous, dramatic difference.

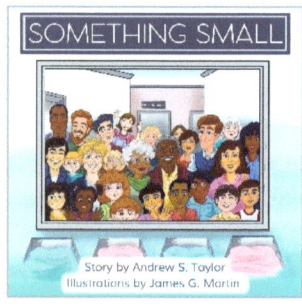

Author Andrew S. Taylor and Illustrator James G. Martin subtlety show how the small, individual items, fantastically fit, into the big, beautiful, perfect picture. And so positively prove, everything and everyone, in our most wonderful world, most definitely and decidedly, matters!

A Cloud & The Eye of the Beholder

Within these poignant pages, we will explore how one sees... a cloud. Do you adult-ly and definitively define a cloud scientifically, as an accumulation of water vapor? Or do you child-ly and simply see a bunny's cottontail or a dramatic dragon's spiny sail? And maybe, most importantly, can you see both these things, both at the same time? YES! YES YOU CAN!

Author Andrew S. Taylor and illustrator James G. Martin delicately depict how we gradually grow up, seeing the world based on our beholder's eyes. They simply show how one should always sing and dance in all the puddles one can find. And how, with both eyes open, one should always anticipate all the rainbows and sunrays, which will soon break through the clouds, and illuminate your life!

Mommy, Am I BEAUTIFUL?

Within these poignant pages, a lovely little girl learns the life lesson of what is really the difference between being *externally*, purposely pretty, and *internally* doing the long list of high-quality character traits that make up the word BEAUTIFUL. As her older sister is getting ready for Prom, she is sent to learn this life lesson from Mom, the same way it has been passed down through generations.

Author Andrew S. Taylor and Illustrator James G. Martin address the intrinsic and introspective idea, in storybook form, that beauty comes from the inside. Whether it be her first day of school or for a special occasion, like a picturesque Prom, what matters most is what she is internally made of, and what are the core content qualities, of her truly confident character.

LULLABY-ed Child

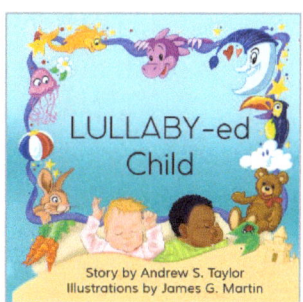

Within these poignant pages, are fantastic frames artistically availed and rightly ready for fabulous photos. And also, the tender text is a simply sweet, lovely LULLABY sublimely set to melodic music. Use the professionally provided sheet music for yourself or hear the author sing it using a digital download. And for sure, your child will surrender to serene sleep.

Author Andrew S. Taylor and Illustrator James G. Martin colorfully create a new type of children's book. They provide a soft song to sing and cutely color-full frames, for you, the reader, to fill with your child's family photos. So, if (or when) digital technology, computers, the cloud, or our phones fail, your life's magical memories can be tangibly taken and productively put into a very real, picturesque place.

Sitting in the Lap of Love!

Within these poignant pages, is a short and sweet story of a magical memory: Mom making the safest of all spaces, a loving lap. Every year Mother's Day is in mid-May. With this book you can say, "It is every day!" The author shouts out a big, "THANK YOU!" to his mom. And you too, can simply show and greatly give gratitude to your mom. Or you can say these same sentiments to your daughter, daughter-in-law, any already mom, or any very-soon mom-to-be.

Author Andrew S. Taylor and Illustrator James G. Martin write right words and put into perfect pictures a love-full wonderful walk down a little lad's and a magnificent Mom's memory lane. They set the scene and all is seen. And yes, this book may be dedicated to Andrew's mom, but it is also a necessary nod to all nice neighbors, grandmothers, Mr. Moms, and noteworthy nurturers who help children feel soulfully safe and beautifully beheld.

Every Day is Mother's Day: Sitting in the Sunroom of My Sweetest Sanctuary

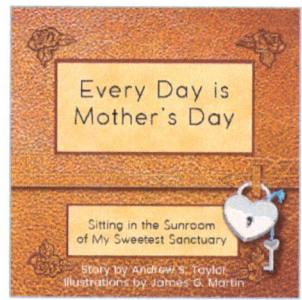

Within these poignant pages, is the subsequent sequel to *Sitting in the Lap of Love!* It is also a perfect prompt to start the art of scrapbooking. Just as *LULLABY-ed Child* provides places to put pictures, this book showcases small spaces for short sentimental stories. Mother and child can beautifully begin here, and lovingly learn, how to continue co-creating, happily-for-fun-ly, and forever-ever-after.

Author Andrew S. Taylor and Illustrator James G. Martin positively present a pair of books as beautiful bookends. The first book was set in the past. This second book is set in the present. Which makes it the greatest of gifts, for one to gratefully give, to your favorite, fantastic, miraculous mother. And as the art of scrapbooking can be a crafty activity that lasts for lifetimes, once started, mothers and children can share memories for millenniums.

A Perfect Day!

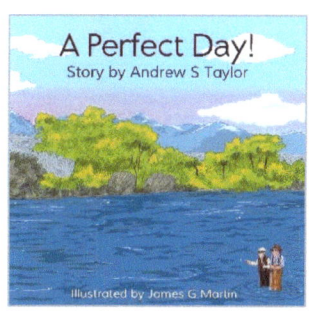

Within these poignant pages, is the origin story of one of my long-lifetime's most outstanding occupations: FISHING! Showing how it's always beyond its best when done with my Dad! I was eight years old, when I caught my first fish. Dad set up, showed, and explained everything. With my success, I was hooked! When I turned a teen, we went to Montana. It was my first "Only-US fishing trip." This is that sweet story.

Author Andrew S. Taylor and Illustrator James G. Martin tenderly tell and soulfully show a time-honored tradition: Father and son going fishing. And just like the movie *Field of Dreams* inspired countless calls of, "Hello Dad. Do you wanna have a catch?," they hope this book will cast out all its lines and catch hold of all angler hearts all around the world. They hope it inspires grandparents, parents, sons, and daughters to all find time to go fishing together, make magical memories, and ALIVINGLY live as many picturesquely Perfect Days as is pleasantly and positively possible!

Another Perfect Day! Every Day is Dad's Day

Within these poignant pages, is decades down the rivers' bends, making more memories and never knowing how (or when) the story ends. And after almost forty years it is that final fact that makes each newly made, magical memory so much more meaningful. For me, fishing is a soul-full-filling summer season. And family, friends, Mom, and Dad, are an all-day-every-day attitude of gratitude! THANK YOU FOR MY LIFE & MY LOVE!

Author Andrew S. Taylor and Illustrator James G. Martin now conclude their collection of ten children's books. (More might be made as ideas arise: coloring books, activity books, and children's coaching books.) But it's this final fishing book that's their last cast of this life's season of super sensational, successful stories. What comes next? Let's see what we can catch, using the inter-net! To You: Good Luck! & FANTASTIC Fishing!

Photography Credits

Unless otherwise specified, the credit includes all photographs on a page.

Andrew S. Taylor, used with permission
Pages: 15, 28, 65, 148, 151, 288

Carole A. Fletcher, used with permission
Pages: vii, 14, 17, 23, 27, 30, 34, 35, 42, 45, 51, 52, 57, 64, 79, 87, 93 (middle), 99, 102, 106, 113 (bottom right), 118, 136, 158, 162, 190, 201, 213, 242, 245, 291, 299, 300, 301

Miscellaneous

Page ix - Daniel Stockman, Wikimedia

Page xvii - Tim Wildsmith, Unsplash

Page 22 - Kristina Edstrom, GPP

Page 76 - Alexander Van Driessche, Wikimedia

Page 93 - left Lorenzo Spoleti, Unsplash; right Rick Vos, Unsplash

Page 97 - Lisinski, iStock

Page 101 - Kristina Edstrom, GPP

Page 113 – Eric Isselee, Adobe stock (top left); Linas T, Adobe stock (top right); Rita Kochmarjova, Adobe stock (bottom left)

Page 123 - Nico Cavellini, Unsplash

Page 155 - Joshua Woroniecki, Unsplash

Page 175 - Skynesher, Unsplash

Page 193 - James Brey, iStock

Page 203 - Chrissy Jarvis, Unsplash

Page 225 - Jacob W. Frank, Wikimedia

Page 236 - Yair Haklai, Wikimedia

Page 246 – Vulcanus, Adobe stock

Page 302 - Vlacheslav Argenberg, Wikimedia